FORGIVENESS

Journey to a Clear Place

M. Lori Torok

FORGIVENESS
Journey to a Clear Place

Reclaim Your Energy, Raise
Your Frequency, and Heal the
World with Forgiveness.

First published in 2023 by Eighth Ray Publishing

ISBN 979-8-9881057-0-1

This book is not intended as a substitute for the medical advice of physicians or mental health experts. The reader should regularly consult a physician or mental health expert in matters relating to his/her health and particularly with respect to any symptoms that may require diagnosis or medical attention.

First edition 2023

Printed in Temecula, California,
United States of America

EIGHTH RAY
PUBLISHING

For Zoë Elena,
Pallas Athena,
and all who have the power
to transform this world.

Contents

Table of Illustrations   xii

Prayer for a Book About Forgiveness   xv

Introduction
The Geometry of the Self   **1**

A Meta4 4 4giveness   3

The Four Lower Bodies   5

How this Book is Organized   8

The 4GiveNess Project: A Five-Week Mystical Journey   10

About Activations   10

The Wide Margins in Life (and this Book)   11

How to Journey Through this Book   11

Part I
The Mental Body: Our thoughts about forgiveness

Chapter 1
What does it mean to truly forgive?   **17**

The Perception of Pain   20

Activation: Acknowledging Pain   23

Phantom Pain, Spooky Energy, and the Karmic Burden   24

Vibration and the Flower of Life   26

Activation: Mindfulness and the Squared Breath   29

Journal   **30**

The Electromagnetic Field of The Rockettes   31

The Empath's Question: Is This Mine?   33

Case Study: Carol at Costco   35

The Unaware Empath   35

The Law of Forgiveness   38

Suffering and Other Core Ideas About Forgiveness   39

Activation: People Who Forgive Well   42

Chapter 2
Why We Don't Forgive   **47**

Case study: Everything is Just a Thought Away   48

Activation: Shining Light into the Shadows   51

Chapter 3
Holding Space: Forgiving Daily   **55**

    Activation: Return to Self—The Heart Unfolding   57

    Forgiving Judgment: Releasing Peace Into the Field   58

    Activation: Working with Loving Thoughtforms   60

Chapter 4
The 4GiveNess Project   **65**
Week 1   **65**

    Meditation   **66**

    Meditation Response   **69**

    Activation: Living in the Garden   70

PART II
The Etheric/
Memory Body

Chapter 5
Healing Systems: Forgiving the
Bigger Stuff   **77**

    Chakras and The Integration of the Etheric Body   78

    Activation: Movement Exploration of the etheric body   80

    Journal Prompt   81

    Forgiveness and the Etheric Body   82

    Activation: Scanning the Etheric Body   83

    Karma and Generational Healing   84

    Tales of Inheritance   86

    Prayer for the Family Tree   87

    Activation: Dance of the Etheric Body   88

    Twenty Aspects of the Etheric Body   89

Chapter 6
The Alchemy of Apology, Forgiveness, and Ho'Oponopono   **93**

    B.L.A.M.E. and S.H.A.M.E.   94

    Activation: Eight Breaths—The Lens of Forgiveness   96

    Ho'Oponopono   96

    Ho'Oponopono Variation   98

    Activation: Walking Ho'oponopono   98

    Activation: Meditating with Ho'Oponopono   99

Chapter 7
Reiki and Forgiveness   **103**

Reiki Sessions for Self-Healing and Forgiveness   106

The Angels of Forgiveness: A Lesson in
Religions and Rainbows   107

Working with a Reiki Practitioner   109

The Wisdom of Detachment   111

It's Time to Set Everyone Free   111

Activation: Reiki for Forgiveness   113

Chapter 8
The 4GiveNess Project,   **117**
Week 2   **117**

Meditation   **117**

Meditation Response   **122**

Activations:

Living in the Truth   123

Part III
The Physical Body: The Elements and the Elementals

Chapter 9
Sacred Fire   **129**

The Invitation of the Mystic   130

Sacred Fire Energy   131

The Color of the Flame   133

The Violet Flame   133

Activation: Fire of Forgiveness   134

Chapter 10
Sacred Air   **139**

Calling In Energy with the Air   140

Activation: "I Am" Clearing the Air   140

The Forgiving Thoughtform   142

Activation: The Forgiving Thoughtform   144

Chapter 11
Sacred Earth   **149**
   The Earth Star Chakra and Your Thoughts   150
   Working with Crystals, Minerals, and Gems   152
   Forgiveness and Essential Oils   155
   Activation: Forgiveness and Mother Earth   158

Chapter 12
Sacred Water   **163**
   Gem Baths   164
   Gem Elixirs   165
   Flower Essences   166

Chapter 13
The 4GiveNess Project,   **171**
Week 3   **171**
   Meditation   171
   Activations: Journeys to Forgiveness   175
   Sunset Journey   176
   Waning Moon Journey   176
   Willing to Forgive   177
   Cutting Cords   178
   Journal   179

PART IV
THE EMOTIONAL BODY

Chapter 14
Sound, Forgiveness, and the Emotional Body   **185**
   Activation: Toning   189
   Activation: Call and Response   190
   The Call from Within   191
   Entraining to the Music of the Universe   193
   The Frequency of Forgiveness   196
   Activation: 639Hz Frequency   196
   Activation: Forgiveness Playlist   198
   The Sound of Laughter   199
   Activation: Laugh Laboratory   200

Chapter 15
The 4GiveNess Project   **205**
Week 4   **205**
    Meditation   **206**
    Meditation Response: **211**

Chapter 16
The 4GiveNess Project   **215**
Week 5   **215**
    Meditation   **216**
    Meditation Response   **219**
    Activation: Be-Coming Forgiveness   220

Chapter 17
Afterward: Forgiveness Activism   **225**
    Forgiveness in My Story   225
    Forgiveness in Your Story   226
    Forgiveness in the World   228

Glossary of Metaphysical Terms   **233**
Bibliography   **241**
Index   **247**
Gratitude   **253**
About the Author   **255**

Table of Illustrations

Figure 1: Line drawing of the icosahedron (M. Lori Torok and Eloku/Canva.com)

Figure 2: My Icosahedron (Photo: Anne Watson)

Figure 3: Matryoshka, Russian nesting dolls (Robin.ph/ Shutterstock)

Figure 4: Rings of energy resonating around the physical body (DeoSum/Shutterstock)

Figure 6: Icosahedron (Photo: Anne Watson)

Figure 7: The electromagnetic field, moving in the torus pattern. (Tyrone da Gama/Shutterstock)

Figure 8: The interconnectedness of the electromagnetic field, creating a unified field of energy. (Tyrone da Gama/ Shutterstock).

Figure 9: Image depicting vibrational resonance with tuning forks (Designua/Shutterstock)

Figure 10: The overlapping space created between two equal circles is called the Vesica Pisces (Piscis), meaning the bladder of the fish. In metaphysical studies and religious symbolism, this is known as the universal womb or the immaculate concept, where Divine perfection resides (artwork: Tyrone da Gama/Shutterstock)

Figure 11: Overlapping electromagnetic fields creating the Flower of Life (Peter Hermes Furian/Shutterstock)

Figure 12: Icosahedron (Photo: Anne Watson)

Figure 13: Energy centers of the body, known as chakras (Space Wind/Shutterstock)

Figure 14: The chakra system in relation to the energy field surrounding the body (Zanna Art/Shutterstock)

Figure 15: Wheel of forgiveness (M. Lori Torok/Canva.com)

Figure 16: A prayer for forgiveness, inspired by Ho'Oponopono (M. Lori Torok, with artwork by Benjavisa Ruangvaree/ Shutterstock)

Figure 17: Image of a Reiki session (Dragon Images/ Shutterstock)

Figure 18: Image of a self-healing Reiki session (New Africa/ Shutterstock)

Figure 19: Image of a Reiki Attunement (Microgen/Shutterstock)

Figure 20: Rainbow over our house, December 18, 2013 (Photo courtesy of Steve Torok and the Angels of Forgiveness)

Figure 21: Icosahedron (Photo: Anne Watson)

Figure 22: The element of fire, as represented in the Platonic solid pyramid. (Magic Pictures/Shutterstock)

Figure 23: Rudra Mudra, a hand gesture associated with the opening of the Solar Plexus chakra/Manipura, the fire center in the area above the navel (D. Things/Shutterstock)

Figure 24: The element of air as represented in the Platonic solid octahedron. (Magic Pictures/Shutterstock)

Figure 25: The Forgiving Thoughtform (M. Lori Torok)

Figure 26: The element of earth as represented in the Platonic solid cube. (Magic Pictures/Shutterstock)

Figure 27: Grounding as the intersection of space and time, or here and now (M. Lori Torok)

Figure 28: The element of water as represented in the Platonic solid icosahedron. (Magic Pictures/Shutterstock)

Figure 29: Waning moon. (Lukasz Pawel Szczepanski/ Shutterstock

Figure 30: Icosahedron (Photo: Anne Watson)

Figure 31: The element of sound/aether as represented in the Platonic solid dodecahedron. (Magic Pictures/Shutterstock)

Figure 32: The rise and fall of emotional frequencies (Ioat/ Shutterstock)

Figure 33: The vibrational axis of the chakral column (Irina Ashpina/Shutterstock)

Prayer for a Book
About Forgiveness

Dear Mother-Father God,
I pray for Your guidance, wisdom, strength, and love
to create, with You and for You,
a book that will assist many
on the path of forgiveness.

Please allow the ideas and words to flow
in such a way that they reach the
hearts, minds, and bodies
of sincere seekers who wish to become
free of judgment, resentment, and non-loving
vibrations in their lives.

May their individual release
from attack, in turn, free myriads of beings
who have been bound by unknown
karmic burden, entwined with cords of unforgiveness
throughout all time.

May the hearts and minds of humanity
be uplifted to allow for expansive healing
throughout generations and lifetimes,
by Your grace and will.

May all be forgiven.
May all be free in Your light and love.

In gratitude, I sing,
Aum Amen

forgive (verb)

for·give | for·giv

1 a: to cease to feel resentment against (an offender)
transitive noun: for·giv·ness
etymology:
In Old English, forgiefan/forgiefenes meant to give up the desire or power to punish.
In Middle English (early fourteenth century), the word became forgift.

Introduction

The Geometry of the Self

I have a quartz crystal in the shape of an icosahedron that is large enough not to lose but small enough to fit in the palm of my hand. As an energetic organism, the icosahedron came to my awareness during my studies of sacred geometry and my investigation of the true meaning of forgiveness. During this time, I began to learn about the vibrational energies of the Platonic solids. In Ancient Greece, Plato hypothesized that these three-dimensional polyhedrons created the classical elements (fire, air, earth, water, and aether).

Since my metaphysical introduction to the icosahedron, I have been inexplicably drawn to its energies. This structure has twenty flat sides or faces, twelve vertices/points/facets, and thirty edges. In the world of the Platonic solids, the icosahedron holds the energy of water and the quality of **Divine** Wisdom. For anyone sensitive to frequencies, it is the vibration of love.

One day, more than a decade ago, I was meditating with this lovely quartz specimen when I was told/shown that we are a lot like the icosahedron—we each have twenty faces and twelve facets to our being. I was also told that by looking through the side closest to you, you can see many of the other sides or faces but

Figure 1: Line drawing of the icosahedron (M. Lori Torok and Eloku/Canva.com)

*Figure 2: My Icosahedron
(Photo: Anne Watson)*

not all, and not the structure in its entirety. Every face relates to the others, connected by its edges and facets, but by itself, it is two-dimensional and incomplete—a mere triangle. I was shown that the other geometric shapes of the Platonic solids are held within the icosahedron. This can happen only because of its many sides. What a loss it would be to the entire structure if even one of those facets were to loosen or if even one of the faces no longer reflected the light.

The play of light on and within the multidimensional structure allows us to go within, to see the depth and relationships of the faces, edges, and vertices. My small quartz icosahedron has a few inner cracks and inclusions, as shown in the photo (see figure 2). As I gently move and shift my friend, I see various scenes come to life: feathers, dragons, majestic white mountains rising and falling, blessed by misty rainbow angels. When light meets these inner surfaces, a mystical wonderland unfolds. Rainbows have been known to live within my crystal friend.

These cracks do not come up to the surface. The surface remains pristine, smooth, and clear. This is considered a crystal of high quality. These deep inner wounds are evidence of change, temperature, and untold pressure. Although I have not documented these changes, some of these shifts and changes within my icosahedron have come after intense meditative experiences; as each experience creates its own changes within. This reminds me of Rumi's wisdom, "The wound is the place where the light enters you."

A Meta4 4 4giveness

Throughout the book, I will share pictures of my icosahedron. Even as I share many angles and perspectives, you will not be able to get the entire energetic landscape of this particular icosahedron. It is also true that, no matter how much or how little I share my personal stories, the inner landscape is evidence of change, temperature, and pressure over time, and we really can never see the whole of it. I am deeply aware that my experiences were and are only a few faces on the icosahedron. The people I knew could share only that part of them that was there for me to see, and my perspective could never encompass the whole truth. Those are the limitations of human life. We are bound by incomplete perceptions, fuzzy perspectives, and the physical limits of time and space.

I am aware that my memories and the stories I share in this book are from a personal and limited perspective about beautiful people capable of much light, texture, and color—who could show only one face at a time. There is so much more to each of us. I write with full acknowledgment that my personal experience of any one person is only that—one or two faces of the whole icosahedron.

I write from a limited perspective; no matter how I move and shift the pieces of my memories and the vibrations, the inner landscape reveals new angles of light and shadow beneath the twenty faces, thirty edges, and twelve vertices. I forgive myself for not being able to see it all. It is not ours to see all at once as humans of limited perspective. I forgive my friend, the icosahedron, for not being perfect inside and out. I forgive the world for keeping secrets and not revealing all faces, edges, and vertices so I could stop guessing, reacting, supposing, judging, and hurting.

Finding peace within this limited structure of being human has come from years of work with the inner ideas and outer actions of forgiveness. I have remained committed to uncovering a deeper metaphysical understanding of the true meaning of, and the real actions of, forgiveness. It has been a life-long journey of compassion (for myself and others) with the beautiful guidance of my angelic teachers (chohans), who are collectively named for the purposes of this book, the **Angels of Forgiveness**.

One of the first times in my adult life I received direct guidance from the Angels of Forgiveness was in meditation. I asked how to let go of the pain I felt from someone who had treated me harshly when I was young but (I knew) would never even consider asking for forgiveness. During the meditation, I was lifted, in my consciousness, to a space above my body, above the Earth. I was shown a few brief moments of multiple cases of abuse, in different forms, at different times, from various people, and even how the energies continue to resonate in my life today. I saw how this pain kept repeatedly returning, in how I felt about myself and how I allowed others to treat me, even as an adult. For a brief moment, I felt even worse. However, the Angels of Forgiveness came to each side of me and lifted me higher. I heard deep within my being, "No matter how you believe you have been hurt by others, it is nothing compared to how you continue to hurt yourself. Your treatment of yourself is far worse than what you have received from any other person. When will you set yourself free?"

This was a profound shift in my understanding. It turned the story I kept telling myself about my past upside down. Could it be true? Was my self-critical nature far worse than what I had received? Were my harsh self-talk and lack of self-care a form of self-abuse? I realized that no matter where I thought it began, it was up to me to change this pattern.

This is how I first came to understand that superficial forgiveness, as it is practiced in so many ways, is a lovely idea as a form of choice. Still, there are actions and changes within each of us, in our daily lives, in these living-energy bodies that are required in order to truly set yourself free, thereby releasing others from the hold they have on you by not truly forgiving. In other words, we forgive others, not because they have asked for it, but because we need to be free from the past. Otherwise, we will carry this pain from one moment to the next moment, to the next, and so on, until we activate authentic forgiveness.

For me, this feels like getting *inside* the icosahedron rather than remaining on the surface. The icosahedron is yours. In fact, you are required to remain in the center of your being rather than looking for yourself inside someone else's geometry.

From that moment on, I became a student of the Angels of Forgiveness, my teachers. They are not all Angels; they cross a few different realms in the Spiritual hierarchy, including Archangels, and **Ascended Masters, Chohans** of all sorts. They are quite comfortable being called by the term "Angel," as in this context, it refers to a being who is a Divine Messenger. They continue to assist with this work and may have even led you to *find* this book for your mystical journey to the clear place. Are you ready? Let's get started.

The Four Lower Bodies

To be in embodiment means that you are a spiritual being having a human experience in a physical body. This physical body is made of matter, meaning material density. Matter has weight and fills space. We are configurations of electrons that make up atoms, which construct all forms of physical life. Science has been focusing its collective attention on the journey within, going smaller and smaller into the particles and waves of atomic and quantum biology. Yet, there is much to learn about the outward human anatomy beyond the skin, moving out into the electromagnetic field around us. This intangible science requires us to be sensitive, literally engaging our other senses rather than working solely with the visual cortex to observe and analyze matter.

Throughout my life, I have been highly sensitive and empathic, feeling the energies in the field beyond my organic physical body and, quite often, unaware that the energy was not coming from within but from "outside." That being said, it is probably a good time to note that the distinction between inside and outside suggests that we are separate from each other and our surroundings. I have discovered that this is not true. We are much more connected than we are aware of, especially if we are distracted by the appearance of a physical body, which would make us believe that that is who we are. Yet, we know that we will someday leave this body behind. My experience has taught me that the spirit will go on after we leave the body at this lower vibrational plane. We are not contained inside this body, even while we are alive. My work as an energy healer has taught me that there is a field of (what we may call) energy that flows around and through us. This energy is us, and it is connected to each of us. This shared energetic connection makes us, actually, one.

Theosophical Mystics, perhaps first recognized as such with the work of H. P. Blavatsky, have described the wholeness of our individual being as having multiple "bodies," or sheaths of energetic substance, like rings resonating outward. You may find it helpful to imagine it like a series of Russian nesting dolls, one inside the other, as shown in figure 3.

Blavatsky taught that this is an auric egg, with the outer three layers connected to the universal or causal body. In my work, I have found that the energetic structure surrounding the physical body is far more fluid, interconnected, and alive in movement and flow.

The physical body, being the densest, is surrounded by a light/memory body called the etheric body. The etheric body is a spiritual wave-like property that flows from within the physical body outward to the other subtle bodies. They are not

Figure 3: Matryoshka, Russian nesting dolls (Robin.ph/Shutterstock)

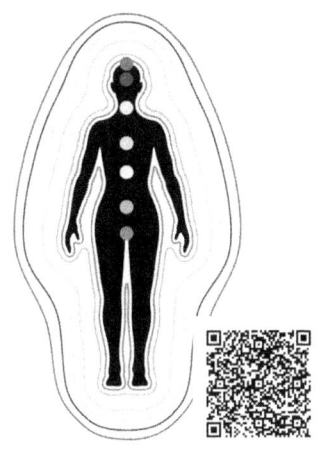

Figure 4: Rings of energy resonating around the physical body (DeoSum/Shutterstock)

defined by hard edges—just as our healthy **chakra system** is not. There is a flow of animating, effervescent, or leavening substance that moves freely through and among these octaves of energy. I see them as waves, like heat moving the air above a flame. The etheric body and its vibrational patterns move beyond the physical density.

Moving outward, the next octave of energy is the mental body. As your thoughts resonate outward, carrying your intentions into the outer world, they magnetize **thoughtforms** held in the personal atmosphere, bringing back the information, whether true or false, into the circumference of your being.

Figure 5: This is an excellent depiction of the etheric body by Arthur Rackham, 1917, in The Romance of King Arthur, *by Alfred Pollard.*

The fourth octave of the body reaches out furthest and is known as the emotional body. This subtle body has the most substantial influence on our surroundings and within our being. Our

/

individual emotions move outward and return, bringing more similarly vibrating patterns. This is important in understanding the challenge of forgiveness. Because your emotional wounds are often buried deep within (what many think of as forgiveness), you easily find emotional evidence to support your personal pain points through the **Law of Vibration**: Like vibrates like.

Because of this ongoing rippling flow of energies through the field of the four lower bodies, it is exceedingly difficult to forgive the past truly and fully, yourself and others, by simply deciding to. The mental body is just one-fourth of our whole being. Choosing to forgive is a terrific place to start, but to become fully realized, we must also activate the emotional body and the etheric body and ultimately concretize or manifest it in the physical body.

The journey to the clear place of forgiveness is ultimately one of balancing the lower bodies by clearing the fields of unloving and unforgiving vibrations. I have been to the clear place; it is filled with beauty, kindness, patience, peace, and love. I return there as often as possible. I plan to make a home there rather than take holiday excursions. May my journey to the clear place, examples from my own life, my clients' stories, and the ideas, exercises, and activations in this book assist you on your path through forgiveness, bringing peace and more light to the inner landscape of your being.

How this Book is Organized

Forgiveness, real forgiveness—not the superficial practice of "forgive and forget" denial—is a healing process. As with the holistic approach of healing, which addresses the whole person, forgiveness works best when you embrace it with the fullness of your entire being. This book is assembled in four parts, mirroring the healing journey of the four lower bodies in the following order: the mental body, the etheric/energy body, the physical body, and the emotional body.

Part I: The Mental Body will give you a deeper understanding of energetics, the Laws of Vibration, and, specifically, the vibration of forgiveness. We investigate how personal thoughts, words, intentions, and actions inform and influence the **collective field** at all levels. This first section contains spiritual landmarks and a mystical framework for the sacred act of forgiveness. Part I is primarily about the mental capacity to forgive and overcome mental resistance to releasing yourself (and others) from the grip of resentment and non-forgiveness.

Part II: The Etheric/Memory Body offers you inner resources for further development and opportunities for integrative practice. We investigate the growth of the soul and the call to raise the four lower bodies to release **karmic burden** and to live from a place of higher consciousness. This section reminds us that the path of ascension requires a release of judgment and a life beyond forgiveness as we journey to the clear place.

Part III: The Physical Body brings you into contact with the four elements (fire, air, earth, water) and your inherent creative alignment with the **Elementals**. This section offers specific and direct activations for working with the elements in overcoming blocks to forgiveness and our connection to the outer world as we release the misqualified energies of non-forgiveness.

Part IV: The Emotional Body allows us to work with the outer-most reaches of our being, the aspect of ourselves that comes into contact with the emotional effluvia of the outer world most directly. Here, we are given tools and opportunities to utilize sound (the fifth element) healing techniques, toning, humming, and the frequency of forgiveness to shift the emotional density that brings unrest, dis-ease, and dysfunction to our lives.

The 4GiveNess Project:
A Five-Week Mystical Journey

Throughout these sections, you'll find a five-week program of deep soul work called "The 4GiveNess Project: A Five-Week Mystical Journey." There are weekly meditations, journal questions, and prompts to deepen your experience, along with "activations" to help you absorb the abstract ideas of forgiveness into actions, which bring higher vibrations into the world of matter around us. This program can be taken at your inner tempo, without hurry, resistance, or impatience.

This five-week program was originally received in 2018 and shared with my clients as "The 4GiveNess Project." I was guided by beautiful Divine Beings throughout this period and told to present this work to others. They state, "With a sincere heart and dedicated intention, you may call upon the Archangels and **Ascended Masters** to assist in learning what you need to know about karmic burden and the act of forgiveness." Forgiveness sets each of us free—bringing us back to our natural state of Divine Loving Awareness.

> Forgiveness sets each of us free—bringing us back to our natural state of Divine Loving Awareness.

For organizational purposes, the meditations and activities of The 4GiveNess Project are divided into "weeks." However, there is no timeline inherent to this work. Your "week" may be simply a day—as in the case of "Let there be Light"—it may be a season, or it may be any length deemed appropriate, in between. Allow yourself the freedom and energetic flow required to fully experience an authentic shift and to integrate the changing energies of The 4GiveNess Project. Your 4GiveNess Project will be as long as it needs to be. Let us honor that.

About Activations

As well as the five-week forgiveness program, you will encounter practical "activations," which will help address energetic blockages within the four lower bodies. Activations include journal prompts, questions to answer, meditation prompts, artistic expression prompts (painting, music, dance, vocalizations, etc.), or activities to undertake to put action/energy into the abstract idea. Some of these activations can be done directly on the page or in your journal, and others are better suited in/on another space, such as movement or painting, or lived experiences.

Activations are intended to assist you in activating higher consciousness and raising the vibration of the physical world. This is the supportive action behind forgiveness and the seeds of **spiritual activism**. These Activations are designed to help you clear and raise your vibrational frequency into the state needed to flow with the Angels of Forgiveness, your **Higher Self**, your Light Body, and your unique expression of the Divine Presence.

The Wide Margins in Life (and this Book)

You will notice the exceptionally wide margins of this book and the blank journal pages at the end of each chapter, at least in the physical copy of the book. This is to give you a place to reflect, respond, and process the ideas and glimpses of inner scenes which come up (like working with the icosahedron). In some places, there are quotes to ponder or prompts to wend through. Suggestions abound in this inner workbook to assist you on your journey. This book becomes yours as you create a working higher-mind-map to your clear place.

If you are an e-reader, then you might choose to open a fresh journal so that you can record your work as you read this book. However you choose to take this journey, write, draw, make lists, brainstorm, doodle, and color. Do not hurry, for the journey is the clear place.

Do not hurry, for the journey is the clear place.

How to Journey Through this Book

As you know, life is not linear. It circles, loops, and zigzags in unexpected ways (with apologies to *The Good Place*[1]), a Jeremy Bearimy of surprises. It is unnecessary to start at the beginning

1 *The Good Place* is an American fantasy comedy television series created by Michael Schur. It premiered on NBC on September 19, 2016.

and proceed in order, page by page. In fact, some might want to begin by working through the five-week program, The 4GiveNess Project, and then circling back to the text and activations over the next five weeks.

Wherever you decide to begin, follow your inner guidance as to which of the four lower bodies is calling for the most attention at this time—listen to that. Honor your experience and your own twenty faces, thirty edges, and twelve vertices. Like the icosahedron, begin where you are, and follow where the light leads you.

The Clear Place

I am. Instead, I amble
slow heavy steps
in images of images
mirrors in mirrors
revising
marching, mirroring
and striving.
Creator creating create
-or unaware
creations.
Rest.
Still.
Know.
Creator of
circumferences,
confusions,
and convolutions
return
home.
Om.
We are sacred here.
Know our soul,
alighted in Light
so clear,
I am.
Find you, find me,
within
the clear place
I be.

PART I

The Mental Body: Our thoughts about forgiveness

Figure 6: Icosahedron (Photo: Anne Watson)

Chapter 1

What does it mean to truly forgive?

This has been *the* overriding question of my life: "What does it mean to truly forgive?" I mean, *really* forgive—not just to forget about it, but genuine heartfelt forgiveness. Ask this question often enough, and other questions quickly follow: What do we actually *do* to forgive? What do we *do* with the hurt? Where is it supposed to go? If we successfully forgive, does forgetting follow, perhaps over time? Does time really heal this pain? How much time? Or is forgetting a practice of trying not to think about it, so you don't feel it anymore? The questions become even more akin to mental gymnastics and delusion, than forgiveness. If I am practicing "not feeling" something, am I just deluding myself into thinking this is spiritual? If I already forgave the situation, why does it still hurt like heck?

I took this all very seriously growing up Catholic and attending a Catholic elementary school. I felt that everyone else must have already figured out forgiveness. No one was talking about it in any meaningful way. How did I *not* know what it was to forgive? It seemed to be the cornerstone of what (or so I was told) was supposed to be my relationship with God. I was told that God would forgive me to the degree that I forgave others. But I didn't really know what this forgiveness thing was. Yikes! It's even in the cornerstone prayer: "Forgive us our trespasses, as we forgive those who trespass against us."

Clearly, I was supposed to be *doing* something with this beyond my dutiful recitation. At that point, I knew I was in some sort of predicament. I didn't know how to forgive. As a young girl, I even contemplated bringing this to the priest during our regular elementary school confessions, "Forgive me, Father, uh . . . for I have no idea what forgiveness is."

The best I could muster on the forgiveness front was to *not think* about the harmful offense and *not feel* the hurt inside. Is forgiveness, then, a matter of disciplined thinking and repressed emotion? Don't think about it; don't feel it. Surely, I thought, there is more to this than learning to become numb. What must we *do* to forgive?

I had a challenging childhood. Perhaps you did, too—so many of us do. Until recent generations, open abuse of children was somewhat acceptable. Childhood traumas may also be a part of the sacred agreements we co-create for our soul's learning. My childhood, this time around, was physically, mentally, and emotionally unhealthy. I was adopted into a family where anger led the way—chaotic and inconsistent parenting helped to foster hypervigilance, fear, insecurity, and extreme sensitivity. If I misbehaved, my place in the family was threatened, and I was told I would be "sent back" to the orphanage. Although this is not the focus of this book, it is just one part of my icosahedron that will help you understand my perspective. I grew up trying to prove my worth and keep my place in the family.

Perhaps the extreme fear and my tenuous connection to those around me lead me to seek assistance from above and to reach up when it wasn't safe to reach out. I had an Angelic connection and an inner "voice" that regularly and softly "spoke" to remind me that I was not a bad person (despite what I was being told), that, in fact, I was good. While I had been living within what the physical world of matter seemed to be showing me about my challenges, I had the undeniable inner feeling/hearing/knowing that there was something greater within, super-imposed, and beyond this world of the senses. This was a blessing.

On several occasions, I was awakened in the night to see Spirit/ Angelic Beings present in my childhood room, bringing comfort, and being a watchful and peaceful presence. This created a curiosity about spirit and the **inner light** I felt as an undeniable presence in prayer and meditation, even as a young child.

Later, in young adulthood, I would sometimes receive messages from Angelic visitors who guided me with my health and wellbeing. On one extraordinary occasion, I was miraculously transported from a dangerous situation on a deserted winding country road in the middle of the night after my car had run out of fuel. I had been walking for quite a while. A car had stopped a ways up ahead and was waiting for me as I walked along the road. I decided to turn into the next driveway, to pretend that this was my destination. As I began to walk up the unfamiliar driveway, I was brought instantly to safety in a disorienting swirl of something like fireflies and stars. I was suddenly exactly where I needed to be. The next morning, a friend drove me to tend to my car, and we discovered the mystical experience had transported me at least five miles in an instant. Another blessing.

A bit later in life, while I was a Professor at the University of Alabama at Birmingham, I was overwhelmed by the callings from Spirit. It had become difficult to focus on my work in the seemingly "real" world of everyday life matters while experiencing so much information from the other side of the veil. I lived a busy, high-stress material life and a richly-saturated spiritual life. I was accustomed to overscheduling and filling every "waking" moment with minutia that seemed to matter. I was overwhelmed. Out of frustration, I asked the Angels to stop connecting with me, saying that I wanted to live a "normal" life and that it all must go away. I asked them to leave. Later I would learn that due to free will, my request was granted. For ten years, it was quiet. It felt like the phone was no longer ringing, so to speak. I was essentially Angel-free.

I still had a strong meditation practice, but it was different during those ten years. I even "forgot" about how the Angelic connection was such an essential part of my life. When the calls returned, they were stronger than ever, even urgent. By this time, I had significantly changed and was reconnected more strongly. I was told, "The hour is late." Now, I was ready to hold space with the Angels, for the Higher Good, in service to the Light.

I used to wonder "where" my spiritual relationships would be by now had I not "turned off" my reception for ten years. Did I miss out on some Divine Destiny because I looked the other way for too long? Did I make an irreconcilable mistake during that time? These concerns, ranging from worry to regret, are not helpful vibrations, of course. And so, I was guided to make my amends and apologize for that choice, made out of fear, which made me ask for the Angels to leave. I asked for Divine Forgiveness and welcomed my unique relationship with God back into my life. I accepted my journey with great enthusiasm and with a joyful heart. Lastly, I needed to forgive myself for my choices, remembering that in the ten years that passed, I had become a different person and was now better able to work with these energies, holding nothing but love for the process. Thank the loving Creator-God.

The Perception of Pain

We receive information through our five (or more) senses: sight, hearing, taste, touch, and smell. These senses are wired into the lived experience of our physical body. To the degree that our physical bodies are real, pain is also real in the physical world of matter.

I learned early on that the pain I feel in my physical body is an indication or a message of disruptive energies—usually my own thoughts. The thoughts in my lower mind will often mislead me into thinking about things that are not healthy, projecting memories of the past or fear of the future onto and into the physical form of my body.

Once while teaching at a local college, I was walking across campus with a colleague. He shared some thoughts with me about my decision to apply for advancement at the college. If I were to receive this new position, it would be a significant increase in responsibility and financial stability. As so many people do, he was saying some things that seemed supportive, but it was obvious that he did not think I should apply. I certainly did not need his approval or support, but I was open to hearing his opinion. As we continued walking, we came to where he would go in one direction, and I would go up the stairs to the classroom where I was going to teach my class. The last thing he said to me was, "Well, whatever happens, don't take it personally." As I said, on the surface, that is a supportive comment, but underneath, he was also saying that he didn't think I could get the promotion. We departed, and I started up the stairs. I was about three steps up, and my knees were in sudden and severe pain. They were fine one moment; the next, I could not move. I was in agony. My knees had no strength to lift me to the next step. My arms were filled with books, so I couldn't even use the handrail to lift with my arms. I was, in an empty stairwell, unable to move, and I was in tremendous pain.

Because of the sudden and severe onset, without any prior knee difficulties, I replayed my colleague's statement before we went our separate ways: "Whatever happens, don't take it personally." The words were echoing around me. I realized this was due to the negative statements I perceived in our discussion. I had accepted his doubt into my field, the doubt I now felt about myself. Further, I did exactly what he warned me not to do (albeit about his statement, not about the position); I *was* taking it personally.

"What to do next?" I thought. Out of desperation, I began talking to my knees. I said, "I know you were listening to him. But that is just his opinion. I know you're scared. I know you do not feel confident, but we are okay. We are going to do this. Thank you for showing me how scared I am, but we are fine. Forgive me for accepting his energy and sending it through my body. I don't want to hurt you. I hear you. I love you. We are going to be fine."

The pain left as quickly as it came. I got to the top of the stairs. I lifted each leg, swinging the lower leg at the knee. Nothing. I stood there in amazement for a few moments, somewhat stunned. What just happened? Does my body really respond that quickly to my thoughts? Do my body and everything I feel within it demonstrate what I'm thinking and feeling? Is my body also responding to other people's thoughts about me? Can we "talk" to our body, and does it talk back? Can we talk to our pain?

In pulling back the cover on this situation a bit further in meditation, I understood that this man's comments were not the *cause* of my pain. This was not a psychic attack; this was coming up from within me. I was a participant in this energetic exchange. I accepted his energy because I already felt that insecurity and lack of ability woven deep within me. According to the Law of Vibration, like vibrates like. More will be said about this later.

According to the Law of Vibration, like vibrates like.

He was showing me something that already existed within me; it vibrated up as pain, bringing forth something I had buried within myself. It needed to be heard; it needed to be healed.

Activation:
Acknowledging Pain

Pain can be physical, emotional, or mental. Is there something in your past that comes up in your memories as painful? Write about a painful memory here. Describe the situation, whether it was a choice you made (the pain of regret) or something someone said or did to you. Allow yourself to fully describe the pain. What does this painful memory feel like to you?

If this pain lived somewhere within your body, where would it be? If you don't know for certain, go ahead and guess. Where would it be if it were *within* your physical body?

Can you pull off the cover of the situation and go a bit deeper? What is this pain showing you about your thoughts about yourself, about your core beliefs, about your fear?

On a scale of 1–10, how comfortable are you speaking to/with your body?

1   2   3   4   5   6   7   8   9   10

"What are you trying to tell me?" Talk to the pain itself. Try not to get distracted by your assumptions about the pain, where your mind may want you to *think* this comes from, or even your discomfort with the exercise. What is your pain telling you? If you do not have a clear answer, permit yourself to guess: "If I had to guess, this is what the pain is saying to me:"

....

....

....

....

....

Once you have heard the voice of the pain, perhaps even cried some tears, it is time for you to talk to the pain like a loving parent would talk to a scared child. What do you want to say to your pain? Let your pain know you have heard it, that you understand the message, and that all is going to be fine. Practice apologizing to your pain for not paying attention to its message earlier. You are going to be a more careful listener from now on.

....

....

....

....

....

Phantom Pain, Spooky Energy, and the Karmic Burden

When someone has been through the trauma of losing a limb, they may experience the energetic imprint of the limb still being there, feeling the sensations and pain of a missing limb. We call this phantom pain. Unforgiveness similarly presents itself—recalling the vibrational energy of past harm as if it were happening here and now.

Einstein was perplexed by this "spooky action at a distance"[2]—that a part of the body is connected by energetic impulses to the rest of the body over time and space, as if it were present, here and now. Whether you call it phantom or spooky, the idea is the same. It is a real vibrational response to a physical unreality. It is a metaphysical reality resonating in the physical universe. Taking this further, if all of humanity is one, as a child of the Divine Creator, being one, when one of us is in pain or distress, this "spooky" energy vibrationally connects it to the rest of the "body" through all of us.

This is also how you can recognize energetic **cords** to other times and places within the physical body. However, this can vibrate/resonate through you in the emotional, mental, and energy bodies if you have not requalified or reattuned those energies. Even the most beautiful harp can be polished and maintained as a gorgeous piece of sculpture or furniture, but unless the strings are taken care of and tuned regularly by adjusting the tension, the vibrational tones will not create beautiful music. Indeed, the human being is as complex as the musical instrument, more so as it requires attunements to the vibrational planes beyond and above the physical to create its beauty and art.

The human etheric body (energy body) draws in vibrational information from many directions/dimensions. You are both a receiver and a transmitter of energetic vibration (information). This is ongoing and continuous. Energy moves in all directions evenly; it is not a narrow rush of force in one direction only, like the flow of water in a stream.

Consider the electromagnetic field around you. This field sends energy outward (electro), and it draws energy back into its center (magnetic). This is a balance of the masculine and feminine energies within, around, and through you. The **torus** pattern (see figure 7) gives you a visual image to connect the ideas. Science can

You are both a receiver and a transmitter of energetic vibration (information).

---

2 Born, Max. *The Born-Einstein Letters 1916–1955—Friendship, Politics and Physics in Uncertain Times.* Macmillan, 2005. Pg. 155

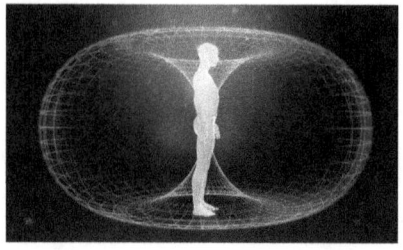

The electromagnetic field surrounding the physical body. Tyrone da Gama/Shutterstock.com

Figure 7: The electromagnetic field, moving in the torus pattern. (Tyrone da Gama/ Shutterstock)

Electromagnetic fields interconnected. Tyrone da Gama/Shutterstock.com

Figure 8: The interconnectedness of the electromagnetic field, creating a unified field of energy. (Tyrone da Gama/Shutterstock).

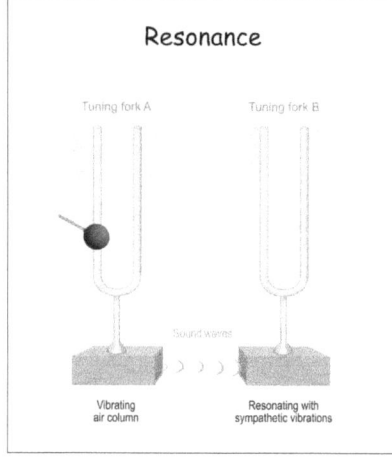

Figure 9: Image depicting vibrational resonance with tuning forks (Designua/Shutterstock)

measure this field around bodies and smaller systems, such as electronics, devices, and even specific organs, like the heart.

Your personal electromagnetic field surrounds the physical body beyond the skin. The field around you is you, as well. You vibrate/transmit your thoughts and feelings outward from your core, out into the field. The vibration of this field interacts and is requalified by those nearby (whether in your physical proximity or in a shared energetic space—like the phone, television, or even a virtual/web-based[3] environment). The magnetic receiver that you are recalls that energy back into yourself, transformed by the experience of what seems like the *outside* world. This multidimensional world operates continually without, for most, our awareness.

Vibration and the Flower of Life

The Law of Vibration is a **Law of Life**: *Like vibrates Like.*

---

3   Notice the term, web.

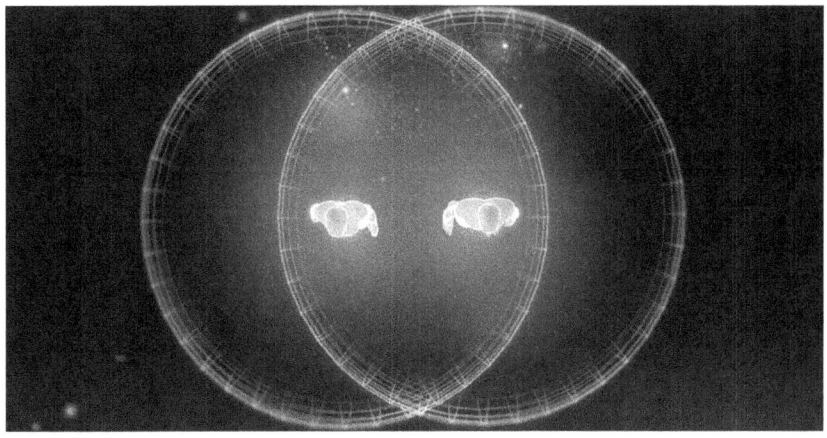

Figure 10: The overlapping space created between two equal circles is called the Vesica Pisces (Piscis), meaning the bladder of the fish. In metaphysical studies and religious symbolism, this is known as the universal womb or the immaculate concept, where Divine perfection resides (artwork: Tyrone da Gama/Shutterstock)

For everything produced—a thought, a word, an action—there is a vibration, a frequency (an oscillation[4] of energy). This physical vibration, being movement, is not isolated in a vacuum—just as you are not—it moves outward, through time and space, resonating with all energies with a similar frequency. It creates a geometric pattern that vibrates the neighboring geometric patterns, affecting the full **Flower[5] of Life**, for *like vibrates like. (See figure 9)*

You are not a victim of someone else's vibrational field but an active participant. Others will show you (in resonance) that which is already within you. This is often demonstrated in sound healing with tuning forks. If you hold two or more tuning forks that are tuned to the same frequency, striking just one of the forks will send the other(s) into vibrational resonance. Each of

Figure 11: Overlapping electromagnetic fields creating the Flower of Life (Peter Hermes Furian/Shutterstock)

---

4 Oscillation is the frequency of a repeating vibration, which creates a pattern.

5 Flow-er of Life

Others will show you that which is already within you.

them will tone. This will not happen if the tuning forks are of different frequencies, for like vibrates like.

Being human and experiencing emotions and challenges of an often-lower frequency, we may, without awareness, send out into the Flower (Flow-er) of Life, the unified collective field, energies of a lower vibration—frustration, anger, and disappointments of all sorts. These are karmic patterns and energies that will need to be resolved, balanced, and healed. As vibrations move outward and around us, they will eventually (sometimes rather quickly) move back toward us, just as every exhale in life is followed by an inhale.

Purifying your part in the vibrations of the Flow-er of Life is a powerful and effective way to help yourself clear misqualified energies and the dysfunctional patterns which move around and through us. There is healing in understanding your participation in the energetic health of the world. Learning to take responsibility for your own energies and engaging in the cleansing of your energy field is an essential step in this process.

Nikola Tesla wrote of our energetic interconnectedness in an article published in *The Century Illustrated Monthly Magazine,* June 1900, entitled "The Problem of Increasing Human Energy:"[6]

---

6 Nikola Tesla, "The Problem of Increasing Human Energy," *The Century Illustrated Monthly Magazine*, June 1900: 175–211.

Though free to think and act, we are held together, like the stars in the firmament, with ties inseparable. These ties cannot be seen, but we can feel them. I cut myself in the finger, and it pains me: this finger is part of me. I see a friend hurt, and it hurts me too: my friend and I are one. And now I see stricken down an enemy, a lump of matter which, of all the lumps of matter in the universe, I care least for, and it still grieves me. Does this not prove that each of us is only part of a whole?"

In the same article, Tesla describes his vision of humankind having the ability to access the intelligent energy of the sun directly in ways that expand their abilities and energies. Your breath demonstrates the energetic interconnectedness of each of us and our connection to the larger field of the planet and perhaps the universe at large. We will discuss this more in the next chapter. But for now, let's take a breather.

Activation:
Mindfulness and the Squared Breath

The air around you was once inside you or soon will be. Your thoughts inform the molecules of the air of your intention. The following breathing exercise is an effective way to work with the breath to clear your surrounding energy field by engaging the living energies of the electrons, to recalibrate the electromagnetic field in Divine Alignment. This is a four-part breath (inhale, hold, exhale, hold), which explains the term "squaring" the breath, with four equal sides.

1. **Inhale:** As you breathe in, bring your awareness to the microscopic light particles within the structure of the atoms surrounding the nucleus—the electrons. These are vibrationally attuned to the energies of the Great Sun and the

Divine Creative Energies of the Great Rays. As you breathe in, connect with the blessing of this light for co-creative purposes.

2. **Hold the breath:** At the top of the inhale, hold the breath in your lungs, as the electrons are qualified/attuned to your thoughts and intentions.

3. **Exhale:** As you exhale, send your thoughts and intentions into the field to create what you hold within your imagination (thoughts) and feelings.

4. **Hold the breath:** At the bottom of the exhale, hold it, allowing the intentions to plant themselves into the firmament of the universe, like sowing seeds in the field of energy.

Repeat the exercise for 10 minutes or longer if it feels comfortable and enjoyable. Take this exercise at whatever tempo feels right to you, paying close attention to the thoughts and feelings that arise. Notice where there is discomfort or resistance to the exercise. With a little practice, you can gain control of your thoughts and emotions, even when the energies around you may feel disruptive. Notice what happens to those disruptive energies as you breathe health and life into the field.

Journal

Which of the four parts of the breath feels smoothest/most effortless for you to accomplish (has the least resistance)?

Which of the four parts of the breath feels the least comfortable? What persistent thoughts or emotions come up for you at that point? Thoughts? Feelings?

If you had to guess, or perhaps you already know, where does the discomfort come from? If you took the cover off the discomfort, is there a subtle, or not-so-subtle, energetic message there for you? What is your breath saying to you? What is the air whispering to you?

The Electromagnetic Field of The Rockettes

As a young adult in my twenties, I lived in New York City and was a professional dancer/singer. For three years, I danced with the Radio City Rockettes. I spent a couple of years on tour with this troupe traveling from city to city performing the classic precision dance routines, which included toy soldiers and high-kicking tributes to frothy Americana, with kaleidoscopic demonstrations of finally-tuned mirror neurons.[7]

---

7 Mirror neurons are brain cells that react when a particular action is performed and when it is only observed. Some scientists believe that the neural basis for empathy may be a system of mirror neurons.

Forgiveness: Journey to a clear place

This was a time of tremendous personal growth for me. Although this work didn't feel like home to me, it certainly provided me with the opportunity to see the entire country, which I wouldn't have been able to experience otherwise. It also gave me much to learn about—what it meant to be a woman in today's world, to be a performer, to be the observed and the observer, and to develop my version of being a human being. This was a special and unique experience.

Looking back through the lens of today, I see that I was exploring the electromagnetic field of the Rockettes and my place within this energetic ecosystem. It's no wonder I was reading much about chaos theory, Zen Buddhism, the healing power of crystals, and Tesla during this time. The path is the path.

One day, I was backstage right, in the third wing, in line (Rockettes usually enter this way—almost always in some sort of a line), when the person behind me snapped a last-minute correction at me. I don't even recall what she said—something I was doing or not doing that she felt she needed to correct at that moment. Under normal circumstances, I would like to think that I would have been able to receive this correction and make the shift with ease (maybe). However, there is a rule among professional performers that the actors/dancers do not give notes or corrections to each other, as that creates a hierarchy and superiority divisions within the troupe. All notes are supposed to come from the director or stage managers. Nonetheless, anyone in this work knows it happens.

That day, I failed to hold my personal space, although I certainly held my tongue. I buried my hurt and somewhat angry feelings. The cue came quickly, perhaps just a few seconds after the note was given to me, and out of the wings, we danced. Smiles. Nothing but smiles in this kind of work. The incongruity of the smile on the outside and my processing of the harsh note I had just received bottled up within me, and I felt something very much like poison traveling through my body. I became unexpectedly physically weak, even though I was used to asking much of my body and pushing onward. When I arrived at my spot and brought my right foot down to begin a jump kick, I felt a surge of electrical pain that chased through my body, from my foot to my head. I continued, finishing the routine and the rest of the performance with quite a bit of physical pain.

Later, x-rays discovered I had a stress fracture. Stress fractures are tiny cracks in the bone due to overuse and muscles that cannot absorb additional shock. Yup. That's about right. According to Louise Hay's brilliant work on reading the psycho-spiritual-physical causes of illness, a broken bone signifies a resistance of authority, and the foot represents your ability to move forward on your path.[8] I also want to bring in the dominant feeling of poison circulating through the body at the time; Hay's work suggests that poisoning, albeit in the case of food poisoning, is a sense of allowing others to take control and a feeling of defenselessness.

This was one of the first times—before the knee pain on the stairs but, indeed, not to be the last—when I *knew*, from deep in my core, the direct correlation to how I was feeling, what I was thinking, and the way it stormed immediately creating a physical symptom or dysfunction. Later, my continued work with dance and dancers would immerse me in the study of energetic psycho-physical-spiritual relationships in mind, body, and spirit.

The Empath's Question: Is This Mine?

My emotional poison was one piece of the equation that needed to be addressed, as it is with many of us. However, not all of what I/we feel comes from the inside. Human beings are far more empathic than we realize. We are constantly picking up other people's energy, overlapping into the vibrations of the collective electromagnetic soup, reacting to that energy, and sending it back out again in all directions around us.

As an empath, picking up other people's energy was problematic

---

8   Hay, Louise, *You Can Heal Your Life*. (Hay House 2004).

for much of my early life. Indiscriminately taking in the more challenging energies (fear, disappointment, frustration, anger, among them) around me left me physically, mentally, and emotionally exhausted and often overwhelmed. Yet, I always thought everything I felt *was* mine. I had never heard the word empathic before.

Equally as important, I was often in a state where I was overinfluenced by other's perceptions of me, always seeing myself in a mirror—perhaps this was from growing up in a dance studio, in front of a mirror—and never quite knowing my own thoughts, feelings, and desires, (from the inside) unless I was alone.

Further, my abusive childhood and my sensitivity to surrounding energies created a perfect storm for people-pleasing—judging myself continually through my perception of what others *MUST* be thinking of me. No doubt, this was a convoluted knot of energy, for how can we ever really know what people think or feel about us? And what does it matter if we did know? It should not affect us in the least. A people-pleaser often can't get there because they are continually adjusting themselves to receive approval from someone who cannot approve or disapprove, not really.

It wasn't until adulthood that I learned to ask about the sudden and severe energetic changes I was experiencing. I learned to ask, "Is this mine?" In asking that question, it would freeze the magnetic pull of the surrounding energy, giving me a brief moment to discern *where* this energy was coming from. Was this my thought? Was this my emotion? Was this a reaction to something? Just a split second was all I needed. In asking the question, "Is this mine?" I was given a moment of grace to requalify the energetic impulse, connect with the truth behind the energy, and connect with its source. From there, I could make an informed choice about what

Is this mine? to do next; it would be my choice rather than a reaction.

Case Study:

Carol at Costco

A client, let's call her Carol, came to see me for digestive issues disrupting her daily life. A series of medical doctor visits couldn't find the source of the pain. After we talked about the triggers for this experience, it became apparent that the stomach pain would most often begin while she was out in crowded places. Unrelated to what she ate beforehand, she would often become ill and be unable to finish shopping, for example.

I heard the word "empathic" come forward (a message from her Angels) and was shown that there were tiny cracks in her auric field (the subtle energy field around us, which contains the electromagnetic field). We then talked about her ability to sense or feel the energy of others. She said that she had always thought she could tell how someone was feeling but that she hadn't given it much weight. I suggested that she may be taking on more energy from other people than she realized.

I offered that she asks inwardly, "Is this mine?" the next time she was overcome by a sudden and severe shift in her physical, mental, or emotional state. During her session, we also did some energy healing for the cracks in her auric field to strengthen her ability to hold her space.

The next time I saw Carol, she told me how transformative that one question had become in her daily life. She was able to identify which energies were not hers to take on. In the end, the stomachaches diminished and eventually wholly stopped.

The Unaware Empath

"Is this mine?" Sometimes the answer is "Yes. Yes, dear one, you are frustrated about the situation, and you are allowing it to shift your emotional state. What would you like to do with this now?" Knowing that you are responsible for what happens next is helpful, as you are not a victim of your emotions.

You are responsible for what happens next... You are not a victim of your emotions.

Sometimes the answer is "No. This is not yours." The next question is the same as the other, an all-important piece: "What would you like to do with this now?" After feeling a sudden and severe energetic shift, if you receive "No, this is not yours." Follow up with the question, "Where is this coming from?" Sometimes the answer is simple and direct—someone standing nearby, the thoughts and fears of the classroom full of students on their first day of class, or the person behind you who is unwell. Knowing that, you have time to make a choice. You could bring a different vibrational energy into the field, flooding it with love or joy or healing thoughtforms or peace. This can calm even the most agitated of energies at a big box store.

We, all of us, are more empathic than you would first think. You are also more powerful than you think because you have energetic options. When you are aware, you are also responsible for what happens next within the energy field that connects us all. What we transmit (send out) is projected into the field; we project love-consciousness or forgiveness into the collective field. The projection of love over all the other lower choices is forgiveness.

The projection of love over all the other lower choices is forgiveness.

The unaware empath, about 90 percent of the human population, the Angels of Forgiveness tell me, has no idea that they are receivers, as well as transmitters. They perceive their lives as a timeline (past, present, future) but nothing more than a sequence of linear events in a world of matter. Newtonian physics gave us the perspective that forces (like gravity and motion) act upon matter. By extension, others act upon us, and we separate and move on as individualized pieces of an earthly puzzle.

However, in our current understanding of quantum physics, we enjoy a new perspective, not only in science but in human interaction. In the quantum world, particles behave like energetic waves. The forces between and among particles—people—become "entangled" and can continue to have a shared field of experience beyond time and space. This is demonstrable in science, at the smallest degree of study, in the microcosmic worlds of electrons and photons. However, being a law of physics, it is operating at all times, at all levels—that is the nature of law.

Empathic people feel entanglements and their effects within their daily lives. And even though some do not yet intellectually know about this law or are not yet sensitive to its effects, it is at work for everyone. That means you are feeling the entanglements of your surroundings—the electromagnetic field of every other person's energetic transmissions—whether you know it or not.

Most people perceive their lives in terms of their feelings and reactions to events without looking at the wider spectrum—the higher octaves, the higher bandwidths. However, *aware* empaths, those who understand that we live in a collective field of energy, may feel like victims of the seemingly "insensitive" masses. Some may even wear it as a badge of honor or rationalize their unregulated emotions and behaviors.

Time for another deep breath here.

The "insensitive" masses are also empathic—it is the very thing that has turned them into "insensitives." They have turned off their receptive powers in favor of living in the physical world of solid matter, a world of external sensory perceptions. They continually look outside themselves for proof of their experience, not understanding that the invisible world, the unseen world, is vibrating through and around them, as well. They, like all empaths, like all of us, are receivers as well as transmitters.

The inner world is directly connected to, and at one with, the external world. Perhaps, taking this further, there is no external world. As one of the earliest Buddhist texts, the *Dhammapada* begins, "All that we are is the result of what we have thought: it is founded on our thoughts, it is made up of our thoughts." We are co-creators of this seemingly indifferent material world, through and to the degree and skill of our mental body. Buddha's teaching suggests that our suffering is because of our attachment to our perceptions of the self. Instead, we are advised to detach from our perceptions of attack like this:

He abused me, he beat me,
he defeated me, he robbed me,"—
    In those who harbour such thoughts
    hatred will never cease.
"He abused me, he beat me,
he defeated me, he robbed me, "—
In those who do not harbour
such thoughts hatred will cease.
For hatred does not cease by hatred at any time:

Hatred ceases by love, this is an old rule.
The world does not know that
we must all come to an end here; —
    But those who know it, their quarrels cease
    at once." [9]

> Forgiveness is a matter of releasing the distance between "we" and "they" in favor of drawing a larger circle around "us."

Releasing our hold on past entanglements, which have led to current discontent, is possible. The answer is not to walk away from those who disagree with us or blame those with different perspectives. Instead, we must shine a light on and truly see what it is within *us* that has brought this false sense of separation forward. In this case, forgiveness is a matter of releasing the distance between "we" and "they" in favor of drawing a larger circle around "us."

The Law of Forgiveness

Without an understanding of energy, resonance, and personal authority, the energy flows from one, onto the next, onto the next, and so on. We pass on the energy we receive downstream. Quite often, this is a lower vibrational frequency. You may have heard, "Hurt people, hurt people." This is evident in personal relationships, family dynamics, work situations, social media,

---

9 Frederich Muller, *The Dhammapada*. (Project Gutenberg, 2017).

generational patterns, and even karmic patterns of reincarnation. And so goes the world.

There is another option, one that is in alignment with the **Divine Order** of the creative principle. Hurt people can, in fact, rise out of the pain to triumph over the misqualified energies and change the vibration of the shared collective field. Hurt people can, in fact, heal people. Sometimes it is the one who has experienced the most painful of experiences that can heal and lead others through that journey of healing.

No matter what I received, or from where, I am responsible for what happens next. What I transmit is what I project onto others and out into the shared unified field. This projection of love over the lower options is the project(ion) of forgiveness. When we choose to bring loving vibrations into the field where lower vibrations reside, we are actively participating in the **Law of Forgiveness.** This is what life is here to teach us, how to send out love over all other emotions. Life is a forgiveness project, a project-ion of forgiveness.

Suffering and Other Core Ideas About Forgiveness

Growing up in a dysfunctional family, anger, resentment, and all other emotional discord directed each day. Emotional outbursts, followed by unregulated behaviors, were the norm. There was *talk* of forgiveness, being Catholic and all, but it was talk at best.

One of my earliest memories of forgiveness-gone-awry was when I was a toddler, maybe four or five years old—sometime before kindergarten. I had done something deemed "wrong." It's funny that I can never remember what I did wrong (not to say that I was a perfect child, certainly not); it's just not part of the memory. The seed of the action fades away, but the reactions resonate onward. Nonetheless, my mother was enraged by something that I did. I was going to be punished. She put my clothes in a little suitcase, bundled me up for the Buffalo winter weather, and pushed me out the side door. She told me to go—letting me know that if I wanted to do *that* (why can't I remember what *that* was), I could not live under her roof. She closed the door and left me standing in the snow with my suitcase. Cold and crying, I was unable to move—frozen on the inside, matching the frigid air of the outside. I refused to leave. Part of me felt that I should, that this was my chance to get out of this. But I was too young to figure this out.

I stayed there, a stoic little four-year-old with tears streaming down my face, wanting her to love me back into the house. I saw her looking through the curtained window of the door and watching me suffer. I also remember deciding (at that young age) that it was my job to suffer so that she would know I loved her. Then, maybe she would forgive me. Forgiveness, like love back then, was something I needed to earn, I thought.

Many people on the planet feel that way. The Hebrew Bible shows us that, in the celebrations of Yom Kippur, or the Day of Atonement, animals were sacrificed to atone for their sins and to ask God for forgiveness for the year. Some still hold to the idea that blood must be spilled, and someone (or some animal) must suffer to be forgiven. Perhaps that is more revenge than forgiveness.

Throughout my growing up, my mother had a practice of giving the silent treatment, done masterfully, I might add, for even the smallest of infractions. This would continue even after I fulfilled the obligation of saying that I was sorry. The silent treatment could go on for over a week, often ten days or longer. The longest was fourteen days. Absolute silence in my direction, in an intimate 1,200-square-foot house, in a family of four, without a word or a glance. I was invisible to her for having misstepped in some way. My twelve-year-old self has some deep scars from this punishment. God and His messengers showed me much kindness during these painful times. I was quietly told this wasn't the way of God.

I learned at a relatively young age that forgiveness is less about the offense or the offender and lies entirely at the level of responsibility of the offended. There is power in being offended. What I also learned was that two people can have significantly different views of what actually happened. My sincere but confused apology could not move her from her hurt, and I could not hurt along with her. I usually just needed to wait out the pain until she could *see* me again.

Throughout this time, I was comforted by my Angels, who continually let me know that I was not alone. They also confirmed that I would not need to do this to my children. From a different perspective, I was able to experience this without internalizing the behavior as something to emulate later in life. I could not remain completely detached from receiving this emotional distress. Still, I was often given Divine Love, Angelic connections, and inner support that carried me along my path of self-healing and forgiveness.

After many years of this treatment, I began to understand the hurt this wove through the veil between us—for me, it was between my mother and myself. However, I have come to realize that we all have these fabric veils, the diaphanous energetic borders of self-created separation within the field.

I had to address my side of the veil, which I used to try, without success, to get beyond—wanting to tear it down. I realized that this veil was less about the destination of getting to the other side. I was also projecting *onto* this fabric my feelings about myself. I was also projecting hurt onto the screen and back into my system, my own **energy field.** It was I who needed to learn to forgive, even if no one was asking for it. For my own good, I needed to stop recalling the attack back into my field and giving it residence within, allowing it to inform my vision of myself.

There is power in being offended, but even more in forgiveness.

Activation:
People Who Forgive Well

Where did you learn your ideas about forgiveness? Who modeled forgiveness in your early life? List three people who influenced your ideas about forgiveness, whether the memories appear to be what you might label as "positive" or "negative."

How did this inform your understanding of forgiveness in your teen years, as your social circle began to include more people outside your family circle?

Suppose you did not have an appropriate model demonstrating forgiveness in your life (or even if you did), is there someone in history or in the public eye that you can recall demonstrating the act of forgiveness healthily or effectively? List them here. If you have no one, watch for examples of healthy forgiveness around you. By setting the intention, you will become more aware, and you will find that which you seek.

In the space provided, or in your journal, write a short note of gratitude, a thank you note, to one of the people above, for their positive demonstrations of forgiveness. This becomes an active, intentional connection with this energy in your life. This is what it means to bless an action. Whether you "know" the person or not, your energetic blessing vibrationally attracts this frequency to you (Like vibrates like.).

Dear,

In Loving Gratitude,

JOURNAL
Messages from the Angels of Forgiveness

Chapter 2

Why We Don't Forgive

As you'll see in the following case study, one of the reasons we have difficulty with true forgiveness is that we think we should be past this. We chastise ourselves with non-spiritual thoughts about our spiritual practice, "I meditate; I do **Reiki**; I pray; I light candles; I walk in nature; I read all the right books; I should not feel this anymore." Then we declare that enough time has passed (not sure what that predetermined length of time should be), done. "Viola! I forgave. Now, on to the forgetting." And the mis-alignment with anti-love is set.

So begins the suppression of our emotional body and the control of the ego mind. If/when the thoughts or feelings arise around or within us, we whisk them away, somewhere seemingly outside of ourselves. However, this simply relocates the energy to the auric/electromagnetic field surrounding us. It becomes the clothing we wear, day in and day out. This will continue until the vibration finds a vulnerable place within the physical body, like an open doorway or a cracked window, where the anti-love can manifest within our body. Perhaps it becomes a simple headache or a muscle spasm, but it can also become an anxiety attack, stiffness in the joints, an auto-immune disorder, a heart issue, or a *dis*-ease of any sort—depending on your physical vulnerabilities and energetic patterning.

Case study:
Everything is Just a Thought Away

A lovely young woman, we shall call her Valerie, came to see me for a Reiki session. She was one of my students, as well, someone who had gone through "The 4GiveNess Project" workshop in years past. She came to me for the intentional healing of autoimmune disorders presenting in her life. She had multiple diagnoses ranging from Hashimoto's thyroid disease, rheumatoid arthritis, and pre-diabetes. As a Reiki practitioner, she didn't understand why these ailments were not "going away" but were increasing in severity.

I noticed she was regularly, if not always, "off" her *earth star chakra*. This chakra which acts as our southern axis, resides beneath the feet (about 24 inches below). Because of stress, anxiety, and other misqualified energies, we are pulled "off" of this chakra/axis. This disconnects us from our innate energy center with gaia/mother earth. The disconnect from the *earth star chakra* misaligns our electromagnetic field and will subsequently stop the flow of energy through all the chakras, and they will close. A practitioner can see/demonstrate this with a pendulum.

If this is a common occurrence that regularly (daily) presents itself, there is a deeper energetic message. In my work with divine channels, i have learned about the power of free will and the connections we—subconsciously or consciously create—within our electromagnetic field.

I asked valerie about her relationship with her mother. She told me she had a difficult/traumatic relationship with her mother and quickly stated that she had forgiven her and completed "The 4giveness Project." In the way she said this, I felt she was stating that she had done the action but did not fully accomplish the change of vibration that comes with true forgiveness. The hurt was obviously still very much present.

I asked valerie to tell me a bit more about her present

feelings about her mother. She explained that she knew that her mother did the best she could, that she forgave her, and that she never wanted to see her again. She said something like, "she has her life, and I have mine. I'm done with her."

I thought how that phrase sets us up for the exact opposite—being "done" with something is often a sure sign that it is continually vibrating through our field, not at all "done," but becoming our undoing.

After assisting valerie in energetically moving the earth star chakra back into alignment between her feet at the base of the chakras column, her whole system relaxed and energized. Each chakra opened, deep breathing returned, and her full life force flowed again. This was demonstrated with the healthy clockwise swing of the pendulum.

Holding the pendulum over her heart chakra, I asked valerie to think about her relationship with her mother once again. Instantly the pendulum came to a halt. A look of surprise came over her face as she saw that her thoughts could so drastically shift her energetic flow to an utter and complete stop. I could feel the tension rise in her abdomen, the restriction of her breath, and the pressure in her throat.

I reminded her that she now knew how to open the chakras by realigning the earth star chakra beneath and between her feet. She closed her eyes and consciously "moved" the earth star chakra back into alignment between her feet as her southern planetary axis. The pendulum returned to its clockwise swing over the heart; the tension subsided; her throat relaxed; deep breath returned. I whispered, "everything is just a thought away."

Everything is just a thought away.

There are many reasons we hold on to non-forgiveness/anti-love, and many overlap in intention. Many of these do double-duty by keeping us from forgiving ourselves, as well. As you read the list below, notice your inner responses (physical, mental, emotional, energetic).

Perhaps you recognize one or two of the following:

- If I forgive you, I am accepting what you did.
- I am too broken or hurt to move on.
- I want you to feel as badly as I do/did.
- If I demonstrate how broken or hurt I am, you will feel guilty, and that will appear to give me strength.
- If I remain broken, someone else will fix me.
- If I choose not to forgive you, I will maintain the power/control in this relationship.
- If I do not forgive you, you will be punished by some outside force (like God) who will vindicate my pain.
- If I forgave you, I would be accepting what you did; therefore, I must not forgive.
- I cannot forgive you because, deep down, I feel I am better than you.
- I choose not to forgive because someone needs to be blamed for how my life is now.
- I cannot forgive because it is not my job to do so; that is up to God.
- I cannot forgive you because I cannot forgive myself.
- I don't know how to forgive.
- I am afraid.

If you had any sort of response to any one of these statements, whether it was a physical sensation, an intellectual gasp, or a pang of righteous denial, go back and read that statement again. Sit with it (or several of them) for a few moments and ask your Higher Self (the ascended part of you) if there is something you need to know about this particular statement.

Bringing these **shadow thoughts** into the light is not an exercise to make you feel badly. However, it is helpful for the healing process if we know what is beneath the surface of the emotion (energy-in-motion; e-motion). It is time to allow the energy to flow.

It is time to allow the energy to flow.

Activation:
Shining Light into the Shadows

1. In the space below or in your journal, make a list of people or situations you have had difficulty forgiving.

2. Perhaps using the list above, or uncovering your own shadow beliefs, shine a light on the reasons you think you may not be able to forgive at this time.

3. Create something. Draw, paint, dance, cook, compose a poem or song—or something else that creates a representation of your inner e-motions—energy in motion—as an expression of these shadows. Without fear or self-criticism, give them their time in the light. Get them out. Hear them out with compassion. Don't be afraid to look at the truth of your feelings. The Angels of Forgiveness tell us, "The Light of Truth will not hurt you—but the shadows will rob you blind." Take some time to create an expression of the anti-forgiveness that you have uncovered for yourself.

4. After allowing the emotions to physically express themselves, without judgment, embrace what you have created, whether it is on the page or in the space. Write a dialogue or a poem, or a list of words describing this expression. What is the energy of non-forgiveness actually saying to you? What is revealed in this exercise? What have you uncovered or discovered?

JOURNAL
Messages from the Angels of Forgiveness

Chapter 3

Holding Space: Forgiving Daily

During meditation with the Angels of Forgiveness, I received the following guidance:

> *"What (you think) you see*
> *Is actually judgment."*

Reflecting on the infinite number of times I am loosened from my center by the gaze of judgment, the hurting beings around me, the indignation of co-shoppers, the rage of co-travelers on life's roadways, the feeling-soup in which I myself find simmering as I read news headlines or try to make my way right through queues, questions, and quandaries, I prayed for assistance.

In the past, these were the times I reacted in a way that was not my intention and was far from my best. In previous meditations on forgiveness, I was guided to release my judgment, to know that I would eventually get over the stress and forgive the person or situation. Eventually . . . This was not going to last for long in my vibrational field, so "Get there faster," I heard.

This made a lot of sense to me, and I spent some time considering how to do that. However, I would invariably get caught up in the emotional qualities spinning me around for far too long, usually disguised as justified complaining, disappointment, or anger. Like many, I would analyze my feelings, evaluating the strength of my anger/discontent by how deep the wound was or how objectively "right" I was compared to the "other." I tried to get there faster by fast-forwarding the inner argument, trying to get to the end of the inner trial quicker—me being the victim, prosecutor, jury, and judge. This sure was a lot of mental energy expended in the wrong direction. And, of course, the final outcome was forgiveness. I mean, we are not talking about life and death situations here—but the small things that come up on the daily agenda for the growth of the soul. I needed to avoid the trial phase completely because judgment was at the center of that misguided exercise.

"What (you think) you see is actually judgment."

After asking for the mental focus to hold the space of forgiveness on a moment-by-moment basis for the seemingly small irritations that arise from living on the planet with billions of other beings who see and do things differently, I was given the grace of a **mantra**. This mantra sees me through those times when I am asked to give more than I can in the moment. When I am involved in making dinner, but a family member needs me to urgently tend to their needs. When I cannot be in two places at once (yet). When I feel overwhelmed, stretched too thin, not enough, or anxious.

See, no one *wants* to go through life irritated and annoyed by others. No one *wants* to lose their connection to their Higher Self and inner light. For me, I find mantras exceedingly helpful. I have made it a practice to walk to the rhythm of a mantra, creating a syncopated soundscape for the time being. When I asked my beautiful Angels of Forgiveness for assistance with the lower feelings of irritation to help me bring my focus back to the loving center of the heart, I was given the mantra below:

*"I am undisturbed
in the light
of forgiveness."*

Simple and profoundly effective. This mantra calls in the light, Divine Light. Light is the centerpiece of this simple statement, and it holds the vibration of the intention by surrounding the speaker/ thinker. Calling in the light of forgiveness releases my judgment in the moment instantly, as it moves my focus from the other person/ situation and the judgment I was holding to my center, where I can hold space for light.

The *I am* statement of the mantra activates the **Three-Fold Flame** within the **heart chamber (High Heart chakra)**, reminding me of the spark of the Divine, already present within, keeping me centered and undisturbed and held within the light.

This creates a field of forgiveness in the light around and through the speaker. This activates forgiveness as a quality of the Divine along the mindful path of intentional living. This is a powerful invocation for anyone wishing to raise their vibration and maintain Divine Strength, Divine Wisdom, and Divine Love on their day-to-day journey.

"I am undisturbed in the light of forgiveness."

Activation:
Return to Self—The Heart Unfolding

Take a moment to memorize the mantra: "I am undisturbed in the light of forgiveness." Then use the following practice to allow the energy to become a part of you.

1. Find a quiet place to sit for 5–10 minutes.
2. Repeat this mantra to yourself, speaking/chanting/toning/ singing the words with your inner voice or, preferably, out loud.
3. "How" the mantra is spoken is not nearly as important as how it resonates within and around your physical body. In your conscious mind, allow yourself to weave this mantra through your four lower bodies: the physical body, the etheric body, the mental body, and the emotional body.

4. See the words and/or sound waves weaving the golden threads of this mantra through the heart of your being and the four lower bodies—physical, etheric, mental, and emotional.

In the space provided, write or draw a response to this activity. Your response may be a list of words or a poem, a few sentences about the experience, or a doodle or artistic representation (drawing/painting, etc.) of the experience. Allow this to expand into whatever expression this wants to take within you. If you want to paint, dance, or sing . . . allow the energy to move you into the honest expression of your light by unfolding the heart and following its loving guidance.

Forgiving Judgment:
Releasing Peace Into the Field

Quite a few years ago, there were news headlines of an international adoptive parent who "returned" their child due to insurmountable emotional challenges and physical threats to their own safety. The child was put on a plane alone and sent back to their country of origin. Reading this story filled me with intense judgment and rage. I even found myself silently declaring that I could never forgive such an act. Obviously armed with my own deep wounds, I suppose I felt authorized to pass judgment on complete strangers in this way and even decided that this was an unforgivable act. In looking at myself, I believed that I was taking a "moral high ground" here—somehow thinking myself to be superior to those parents.

Ten years later, my husband and I became foster parents to a teen girl who was removed from her biological parents' home for her own safety. This was a challenging but beautifully rewarding experience to have her a part of our family for over a year. The most difficult part of this experience was trying to avoid judgment. There were so many layers of external judgment on the biological parents—constant assessment and critical evaluations by social workers, psychiatrists, lawyers, and a judge. Being directly involved in the situation, my husband and I certainly had our personal perspectives and judgments, too.

It wasn't until the final appearance in court, when I saw the many lenses and heard so many interpretations of one story, that I realized the larger truth that everyone here seemed to be trying to do the best they could for everyone involved. In a way, this was loving action—compassion. The outcome could not satisfy everyone here—and no amount of righteous judgment could ever make the hurt and past harm go away. The only thing the judge could do was make a decision. I was grateful the decision wasn't mine to make. Since the decision wasn't mine, why did I feel I could and should pass judgment?

My experience of life and its pain brings me to the understanding that life hurts daily. With pain, many will move directly to blame (if we perceive the cause to be outside ourselves) or shame (if we perceive the cause to be within). I have become much less willing to travel either of these paths. Perhaps in recognizing the pain for what it is and being willing to accept it as a fact of life, we do not feel the desperate need to push it away onto someone else's plate as blame—or bury it within as shame. There is pain, and it does not benefit from my judgment.

Pain...does not benefit from my judgment.

Today's constant connection with public opinion and social media debates make it increasingly difficult to refrain from critical judgment. The shift begins firstly within the individual. The prayer below may assist you in making a concerted effort to release the habitual call to judgment and to replace it with compassionate grace wherever possible. This work, I have found, assists in recalling your personal peace and vibrating that outward into the field.

Activation:
Working with Loving Thoughtforms

Take a few moments to consider those times when you made a quiet (or not-so-quiet) promise never to forgive something that was said or done. As I have shared, these may be things you were a part of, personally, or even those you only read about or experienced second or third-hand.

1. Calling these times forth in your conscious mind, see a beautiful pink and gold light enfolding the thoughtform, cleansing it with loving light from within. Try not to "argue" with the thought or retell the story to yourself, supporting your need to judge. Simply see it as something that still vibrates within you. Shine light where judgment once was.

2. Stay with this image of a cleansing pink and gold light flowing through the situation for as long as you need to until the vibration changes and peace begins to flow.

3. For a deeper experience of this, conclude this exercise by putting an image of yourself within your mind. See yourself bathed in the pink and gold light, forgiving yourself for your judgment.

4. See, feel, and know this light surrounds you presently and moves through the four lower bodies (physical, etheric, mental, and emotional).

5. As you begin to feel the peace of non-judgment resonating through you, you may want to commit to a practice of walking this light out into the world—day by day, step by step. The prayer below may assist you in your walk of non-judgment.

A Prayer for the Release of Judgment

Dear Mother-Father God,
I thank you for where I stand here and now.
I bear witness to life unfolding
and will not look away in difficult times.
I acknowledge that I know only my perspective in this situation.
I do not have all the facts.
I walk in no shoes but my own.
I release my need to pass judgment.
I hold the vibrations of peace and love
for all who will assist in this situation.
May Your mercy and grace prevail,
In gratitude, I sing,
Aum Amen

JOURNAL
Messages from the Angels of Forgiveness

Chapter 4

The 4GiveNess Project

Week 1

To The Garden of Truth

In the first week, you are led through a garden by beautiful Ascended Masters and the Angels of Forgiveness as you take enormous strides toward understanding your individual role in the current collective vibration of the world.

We, as co-creators, have been participating in the events, emotions, and emerging truth of the world, over many lifetimes. It is helpful to remember that you have been a member of the human family for many many lifetimes; you are, in fact, your ancestors. As such, you are experiencing the results of the vibrations you set into motion long ago. You have helped to create the world as it is now. And, more importantly, you are helping to create the world as it will be tomorrow.

In this garden, the outer/physical world reflects your inner states—your thoughts, words, decisions, and actions.

This is not a place of blame or punishment. Hear that clearly. Do not use this beautiful process as an opportunity to blame yourself or others. That would be judgment, which always comes from ego and is directly the opposite of forgiveness. Instead, this garden meditation is an experience of observation and energetic

> You are helping to create the world as it will be tomorrow.

recalibration. It is a chance to release yourself and others from the karmic burden weighing us down—often without our knowledge. The meditation below is a journey into the Garden of Truth. This is *your* garden—and it will appear to you just as you need it to be. Try not to direct the journey from your conscious mind but do allow it to unfold before you from the still, quiet place within. You may not "see" the images . . . but you may feel, sense, or simply "know" that they are vibrationally present throughout.

Take this meditation journey three times during the week or your chosen phase. You will experience the journey differently each time, and you will be able to go further with each process.

Scan the QR code to listen to the prerecorded audio of this guided meditation at any time.

Meditation

1. Sit or lie down in a comfortable position. Close your eyes, and know that you are perfectly safe, in this meditation, with Archangels in every corner of your room, wherever you happen to be, to guide, support, and protect you throughout.

2. Take a deep breath. Release any tension you are holding. Release all apprehension you have about this process. Release all need to direct or control the outcome. Know that this is work for your highest and best good. It will assist in the healing process throughout the planet.

3. As you take another deep breath, connect with the Earth Star chakra (24 inches below your feet), and feel perfectly aligned with the chakra between your feet, centered below you. This energy center acts as your southern axis. Feel balanced on the Earth Star chakra.

4. On your next deep breath, bring your awareness to your **Soul Star chakra** (approximately 24-inces above your crown) over your head. This beautiful spinning chakra acts as your northern axis.

5. Feel the connection between the Earth Star chakra and the

Soul Star chakra. See beautiful white light flowing between them, through you, opening, balancing, clearing all of your chakras.

6. In your mind's eye, place yourself in a garden. It is beautiful and lush. See all the colors, hear all the sounds, and smell the scents of this beautiful vibrant place. There may be animals with you. They are gentle and are there for your guidance, frequency, and energetic shift.

7. As you are creating/exploring and walking through this garden, become aware of your energy, the lovely life force energy of the flowers, the trees, the plants, and the Earth beneath your feet. This is a sacred space. The energy that is coming from all the life that is around you is moving through you, as well.

8. There is a particular flower that catches your awareness. Take a closer look at it. See, feel, sense, or just know its energy. There is a healing energy being held for you within this particular flower. Feel its energy swirling, alive, and connecting deeply within your heart space. This life force energy surrounds and flows through your heart, lifting, clearing, and healing what you hold there.

9. As you connect with this flower and feel it touching your heart, you become aware that this is your garden. Every tree, bush, flower, bloom, and leaf represents the thoughts you have had and the choices you have made. See its beauty, alive, around and through you. Continue walking through this garden, being softly aware of what catches your eye and where your thoughts go as you observe your garden.

10. Take your time as you explore your garden.

11. Communing with your garden, you see that some parts need tending. There may be places that are overgrown and need weeding, or trees that need pruning. This is also a part of you—the thoughts and actions from this lifetime and other lifetimes, which need some attention and will

affect the growth and the health of the garden in its present state.

12. If you haven't already, find a place to sit down. Relax further and feel the connection of the Divine Life Force Energy within your heart.

13. Go within that Divine Heart Space, and ask forgiveness for all you have ever thought, done, or created that has harmed another in this lifetime and any other. It is a special gift being given to you from the Angels of Forgiveness that you will be allowed to release the things of the past without carrying them into the present. Ask that the vibrations of disharmony between you and others be rebalanced, be realigned, recalibrated to the vibration of love.

14. We ask the beautiful Angels of Forgiveness to help us understand our part and participation in this Garden of Truth, as you are ready to heal that which has allowed undesirable growth in this garden. Ask: "Please, show me what I need to know"

15. Allow the vibrational frequency of whatever comes forward.

16. At this time, you may be shown some things from this lifetime, some memories. Or, perhaps, you will be shown things that do not come forward as conscious memories, and perhaps they are from previous lifetimes. Hold them gently. It is for your awareness of your participation in disruptive energies.

17. Allow the vibrational frequency of whatever comes forward.

18. Seeing some pieces brought forward for you is a sacred opportunity to be released—to be forgiven. Allow the following statements to wash through you for cleansing and realignment:
    - "I am sorry for any harm I have caused, intentionally and unintentionally."
    - "I ask to be forgiven."

- "I ask to be released."
- "I ask that my release releases all others attached to my karmic burden."
- "Let Divine Grace flow through this garden, healing the Earth in support of all life."
- "Let Divine Grace flow through me and all my lifetimes, healing my soul in support of all life."
- "I am eternally grateful."
- "I am forgiven."

19. Take another look at this beautiful garden, your garden, and see the transformation around you. Feel the transformation within your own heart. Feel the lightness, and let that light extend outward.

20. Repeat the mantra: "I am undisturbed in the light of forgiveness."

21. Allow time for this shift of energy to flow.

22. With a full and open heart of gratitude, take a deep breath, and feel the awareness of your physical body in your space. Bring your consciousness all the way back in, down to your feet, beneath your feet, to the Earth Star chakra. Balance. Centered. Gently open your eyes to look around you, in the physical. See the physical matter around you as if for the first time.

Meditation Response

When you first "arrived," how did you know you were in your garden? Did you see images like an inner movie-screen projection? Did you feel or sense you were there without images? Did you hear the sounds of the garden/nature? Did you simply "know" you were there beyond the use of your physical senses? Perhaps it was a combination of these. In the space below, write a bit about *how* you experienced your sacred garden.

....

....

Describe FIVE (or more) items (plants, flowers, features, colors, animals, etc.) that caught your attention in your sacred garden.

1. ....

....

2. ....

....

3. ....

....

4. ....

....

5. ....

....

Choose one (or more) of the items above. Expand your understanding of it. Why do you think it was present in your sacred garden? What is the energetic relevance of this item at this time? What message does it bring you? How do you feel about that message at this time?

....

....

....

....

Activation:
Living in the Garden

Experience the following activities *after* you have completed the meditation for the week. You may even want to return to the meditation multiple times this week, to gain further insight and to go deeper into the garden. The actions below are equally important to integrate the energies and intentions of your journey to forgiveness. Blessings to the journey.

1. Plant something new in the earth—preferably something that flowers/blooms. Intend that this particular planting will be connected with your sacred garden of meditation in the "etheric realm" and that it will ground healing energies to the Earth for your own journey of forgiveness.

2. Take a mindfulness walk in nature, opening your heart and senses to the messages around you. Without music, without children or pets, without planned buffers or distractions of any kind, take yourself out into the world with an open heart. Allow the heart space to open each chakra as you connect with all the colors and vibrations of the world around you. Whatever catches your eye or ears (or any other senses) is a personal message. Sit with the vibration of that message and allow your consciousness to expand. You may want to journal afterward, to process the messages you received. This journaling may be a list of words, a poem, a dialogue with your Higher Self about your path to forgiveness, a drawing or a painting, or any artistic expression about the journey.

3. Forgive yourself — really **cut cords** and release all their effects on you — Forgive yourself for whatever you hold against YOURSELF. You are not that person anymore. You vibrate differently now. Let yourself GO. Pay close attention to how you pull yourself back into the lower energies through your thought patterns. What is that? Is there a part of you that resists forgiving yourself? What do you need to do to claim and accept your own forgiveness? Beautiful being, child of God, do that now!

4. The last one is tough. But you really must try. I am told that some will need to take a full week (or longer) to get close to completing this. Journaling may be helpful for you.

Prayer

Dear Mother-Father God,
Thank you for welcoming me back into the Sacred Garden. I am sorry for any harm I have caused throughout my many lifetimes, intentionally and unintentionally.
I ask to be forgiven. I ask to be released.

I ask that my release releases all others attached to my karmic burden. May this karmic resolution ripple outward, bringing us back to the Divine Plan for the soul of humanity.
Please allow Divine Grace to flow through the sacred garden, healing the Earth in support of all life.
Let Divine Grace flow through me and all my lifetimes, healing my soul in support of all life.

I am eternally grateful for the gift of
your forgiveness.

Amen.

JOURNAL
Messages from the Angels of Forgiveness

PART II

The Etheric/ Memory Body

Figure 12: Icosahedron (Photo: Anne Watson)

Chapter 5

Healing Systems: Forgiving the Bigger Stuff

The etheric body is a spiritual wave-like property that flows from within the physical outward to the other bodies, equally on all sides, as well as above and below. The etheric body is pure energy and, like light, holds the energetic imprint of the past. For these reasons, it is often referred to as the energy body, the light body, or even the memory body. There is a flow of animating, effervescent, and leavening substance that moves freely through, within, and around this subtle energetic body. For those sensitive to energy, this may be seen or felt as waves around the physical body.

Figure 13: Energy centers of the body, known as chakras (Space Wind/Shutterstock)

The etheric body is fortified by the energetic life force flowing through the chakra system. Chakra is a Sanskrit term meaning "wheel." I am shown that the chakras are moving energy from the inside outward, like a blooming flower made of fire. The motion is something like the torus. Historically, the chakra system

The etheric body is fortified by the energetic life force flowing through the chakra system. has been represented as a rainbow breakdown of seven color frequencies.

Chakras and The Integration of the Etheric Body

One day in meditation, I was gently asked to refrain from thinking about the chakra system as individual pockets, divisions, of energies; this was the "unhealed system." Further, I was told the healing of the chakra system within the individual body is like the healing of the planet: when all the colors combine in light, we will return to the state of Divine Grace, pure white light. We must shift from the debt-consciousness construct of taking, borrowing, and giving up our disintegrated energetic power. Instead, we must integrate the system and return to the full power of one.

This was an important shift in my thinking. The chakras are interrelated and interdependent on each other. It is one system and maintains the life force energy of the etheric body.

Energy healers work with the etheric body in ways that perhaps others do not. A Reiki practitioner, for example, channels high-vibrational light to clear blockages through the chakra system, which is a part of the etheric body. Figure 14 shows the chakra system and its outpouring of energy into the auric field surrounding the physical body.

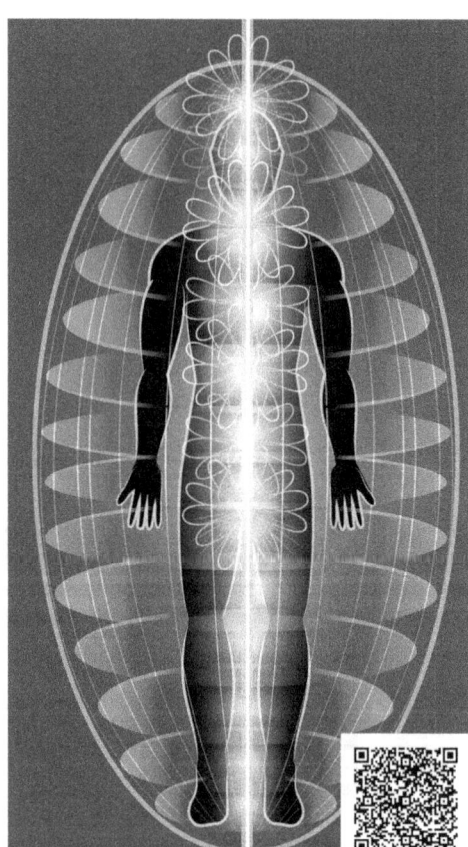

Figure 14: The chakra system in relation to the energy field surrounding the body (Zanna Art/Shutterstock)

The health of the etheric body is directly related to the chakra system's well-being. Notice the white light connecting the chakra system in the image above. Imprint the image in your conscious mind as you work to balance and integrate the full chakral system. Part of the healing of the etheric body is to recall your full life force energy from those areas where it has been taken or unintentionally given/lost. As well, we work to integrate the chakras into the fully functioning system that it is intended to be.

The following Activation uses your kinesthetic sense to "feel" energy flow through your etheric body. The goal is to move beyond the intellectual thought-space and out of the emotional habits we generally surround ourselves with. Instead, you will work from a place of energy body-sensing, the kinesthetic sense.

The kinesthetic sense is the sensation that is communicated from body to body. For example, if you were to watch a video of someone taking a terrible fall, you may "feel" a sensation flow through your being as you resonate on some level with the pain of the one who falls. Although you may feel the physical sensation akin to pain, it is not purely physical, as it is not happening to the observer. It may move outward into the mental body as thought, concern, critical judgment, or even opinion. Further, the sensation may give rise to an emotional response. When you are unclear about your experience of this energetic sensation within the etheric body, it may even feel like you experienced it yourself. This is why the etheric body is also referred to as the memory body. All sorts of energetic memories are stored in the etheric body, which ranges from pleasant to traumatic.

> Part of the healing of the etheric body is to recall your full life force energy from those areas where it has been taken or unintentionally given.

This body-to-body communication occurs all day long, every day. We energetically receive experiences from those on the journey with us. Through the power of digital telecommunications, we even receive signals we are not in direct contact with. These experiences have a wide range of vibrational information, which stays with us, resonating through our being long after the interaction, movie, or social post is removed from our presence. So how do we clear this energy from our field?

For me, movement or dance has proven to be an alchemical and transformative pathway through the etheric body. In fact, other than falling in love, I know no other accessible way to clear the etheric body. It is no wonder Erick Hawkins, pioneer of modern dance in the twentieth century, whom I was honored to have studied with, states in *The Body is a Clear Place*, "Beautiful dancing is . . . always about love told with love which is with the most heightened perception, with effortless, free-flowing muscles that can both feel and love."[10]

Activation:
Movement Exploration of the etheric body

1. Lie down with the soles of your feet flat on the floor and your knees bent. Feel your spine lengthen along the floor.
2. In your mind's eye, see or imagine the chakra column of the etheric body within the physical body. This is a conduit of flowing energy—moving colored lights, if you will—traveling through your body.
3. With an inner knowing or simply deciding, one of these chakra centers is calling for a bit of attention from you.
4. Bring your awareness to this chakra. What is its message?
5. Allow this chakra—this moving ball of light—to lead your body in movement.
6. Sometimes it is helpful to "send" your breath to this area. Allow the breath to activate the movement.
7. Let this movement start small, perhaps with just some rocking or undulation motion, and then it will expand, moving to other areas. Stay with the tempo and pulse of the chakra light.
8. This inner light will lead the way. Try not to push or be impatient with the movement. There is no end goal, just exploration.

---

10 Erick Hawkins, *The Body is a Clear Place, and Other Statements on Dance.* Princeton Book Company, 1994) 77.

9. Release the mental body from its need to control or analyze. Do the same with the emotional body. If any thoughts of judgment or if the inner critic begins to speak up, simply say, "Thank you for being here, but you are not invited to participate in this exercise. I'll call you later, and we will talk then."

10. Return to the light within that leads this exploration.

11. A sense of upliftment and effervescence may lead you to standing explorations of movement. Allow the light to rise and shine through unplanned, unnamed movements which hold an inexplicable beauty.

12. Hold appreciation and gratitude through your exploration, and the light will continue to guide you onward.

13. Continue for at least 10 minutes of focused, gentle movement with your etheric light body, following its impulse.

Journal Prompt

Thank you for taking the time to listen to your etheric body and allowing it to lead the way. What did your etheric body have to say to you? Which chakra(s) seemed to call you the most? Did you receive any guidance as to why this particular chakra was calling to you? What did you receive from this exercise? What will you do differently the next time to work with the etheric body in this way?

Forgiveness and the Etheric Body

For many of us who have worked on forgiving someone or some situation in our lives only to discover that it remains lurking in the background, like a forgotten app taking up valuable memory on your phone, the etheric body is the answer and the solution you seek.

I once heard from a friend after a year or so, without any contact, due to a disagreement about the direction of a shared project. I felt hurt by her words and actions at the time, and I am sure she was hurt by mine. We simply parted and went our separate ways. I did some work with forgiveness and truly felt that I had forgiven her. After a year or so, we decided to get together for lunch. I thought this would be a suitable way to return to some sort of friendly coherence.

During our discussion, she wanted to go back to our prior argument from the previous year. Although I had no desire to pick up the old argument and drag it forward with us into the present, I allowed her to speak what was on her mind, memories of the past. I listened deeply. I tried not to engage in my own rationalizations or past emotions, trying to interject their way into the conversation. Instead, I kept actively sending love out into the field. We concluded the lunch on very good terms and departed on friendly terms once again.

The next day, I could not shake the vibrations stirred up by the conversation. Why didn't I feel better about this lunch and the return to this friendship? I felt that I had *done* everything right. I was owning my vibration, requalifying the energies, and sending love out into the field. I did everything I knew how to do. Why was I feeling so bad? Was this going to take another year to get past this? Will this always remain under the surface, ready to bear its ugly head, if either of us brings it up again? Why couldn't I push this away? I knew this lived beyond my thoughts and my emotions. This resonated within the etheric memory body.

I sat with the Angels of Forgiveness and asked for assistance, and I discovered that the answer lay in the questions themselves:

Sometimes, the fight is kept fresh by the defense against the fight. The answer to the resonance of the memory body is to *release your resistance*. We will often push and resist what we don't want to stay. However, the laws of physics teach us: For every action, there is an equal and opposite reaction. Push, resist, and defend against the energy, and it will strengthen its staying power. Sometimes, we need to let go—drop the fight—put down our arms, and away it flies. And we are free.

The fight is kept fresh by the defense against the fight.

The Angels of Forgiveness directed me to close my eyes and breathe into my light body, and consciously and deliberately "unplug" all attachments. I had this vision as if I were unplugging electrical cords from an outlet within a room. I imagined unplugging outlet trigger points throughout my auric field, cords to pain, blame, and shame. I was releasing all cords. Once I unplugged all the cords, even the ones I couldn't name, I was directed to *allow whatever was left to be*. Be willing to feel it, to hear its vibration. Do not resist or push. Let it flow, and the storm will pass.

At that point, a remarkable vibration shivered throughout my being, and like an electrical jolt, it moved through me and out. A little taken aback, I was told, "Fire, air, earth, and water come together to cleanse and purify the field clear." This is how a storm cleanses the atmosphere. From that moment on, I cannot re-call that energy back into my field, even if I try. It was lifted away, cleansed. I could now meet with and talk to the friend with no misqualified vibration of the past coming through.

Be willing to feel it, to hear its vibration. Do not resist or push. Let it flow, and the storm will pass.

Activation:
Scanning the Etheric Body
1. Sit comfortably for this meditation.
2. Breathe into your heart center and connect with all the love you have ever known, in this and all previous lifetimes, in all dimensions. Feel that love grow organically within your heart center. Love is unlimited.
3. With your breath, the love within your heart becomes a

visible light, shining outward. This light is like that of a lighthouse.

4. From the stability of your core, allow the light to scan outwardly, through your etheric body, all around you, and through you. This light is not blocked by any part of you, including your physical body.

5. Say to yourself, "I am willing to see the truth of everything I am holding within the etheric body."

6. After you say this, pay close attention to where your thoughts go, what emotions come up, and what you notice in the physical body. None of this is random. In this sacred activation, everything is a message.

7. Whatever comes into your awareness is yours to release. Blessing all that comes into your awareness, "unplug" any cords that come into your awareness, holding nothing but love for the person and/or situation.

8. Once you have unplugged all the cords available to you to release, figuratively drop your arms, perhaps literally too. You may even want to shake your hands a bit. Signify that you will no longer resist this energy. Be willing to feel anything that still remains.

9. Breathe. Feel. Breathe. Love.

10. Journal about this experience and anything you would like to process about what you found scanning the etheric body. What has changed for you?

Karma and Generational Healing

Karma is a Sanskrit word meaning action. It is a significant aspect of many belief systems held by millions of believers, including Buddhists, Hindus, and Jains, among others. Karma is demonstrated by the electromagnetic field and the individual's responsibility for every thought, word, and action placed into the field. All misqualified vibrations will need to be requalified; another way to say this is that every discordant frequency will need to be brought into harmonic balance. This is what it means

We are responsible for every vibration we place into the unified field during the soul's journey throughout all lifetimes.

to balance your karmic burden.[11]

All energy that is placed out into the field, your own electromagnetic field, and that of the unified field shared by all of us is the responsibility of the intention, thought, and action of the thinker/speaker/do-er. Quite simply, we are responsible for every vibration we place into the unified field during the soul's journey throughout all lifetimes. The caveat is that many of us repeatedly return to this Earthly plane to work on the growth of the soul and the requalification of the karmic burden without consciously remembering the work that brought us here. To further complicate matters, the world's noise distracts us from the task, as we find it immensely challenging to receive the guidance of our Higher Self and Angels who walk with us in spirit.

Your family of origin is not an accident of genetics; they are part of your soul contract for growth and evolution. You have come into embodiment many times and with the same people in your family circle over many lifetimes. In fact, it is because of the process of re-embodiment through the same family line that you are your ancestors, as well. You have been born into the same family tree many times. What you have put into the tree, both nourishments and toxins, become your fruit in subsequent lifetimes. You are here to heal the tree and to free your ancestors and yourself.

The burden is great, and the hour is late. It is time for us to get on with saving ourselves and the world. Forgiveness is the power to get beyond the lower vibrations which keep us bound to discord, hate, anger, resentment, and self-loathing.

When I was told to create *The 4GiveNess Project,* I was also told that this would ultimately set many people free. I was shown that forgiveness was the piece that many overlooked, thinking it was not their place or within their authority to offer to others or that it

---

11 I am asked not to use the often-used term "debt," here, as there is no real energetic debt. We do not owe anything; no one is lacking in any way. Rather, we are responsible for what has been placed into the field.

was something they did not believe they deserved. And, of course, like so many of us, forgiveness was not something that many knew how to actually "do" or do well.

What you take in as experience becomes ingested, digested, and assimilated into your being. The hurt becomes a part of you, a part of who you are. This vibration moves through your DNA and travels onward—even through generational lines. What you put into the field, in thought, voice, and action, is the karma you bear. Your karma is linked to your genetic makeup because you were/are your ancestors. You have been in embodiment many times throughout your "family" line. What you have sown into the family tree is your karmic harvest in later embodiments. When you withhold true forgiveness, you are participating in the effluvia, the **maya**, the dense material vibration of the collective field.

We begin by taking back personal responsibility for our karmic burden and the personal energy field around us.

We begin by taking back personal responsibility for our karmic burden and the personal energy field around us. Forgiveness acknowledges that you will no longer hold someone else responsible for your karmic burden. You consciously and intentionally release them from your electromagnetic field.

Tales of Inheritance

Families will often share tales of genetic inheritance as stories of potential outcomes. What stories fill your consciousness about your family line? Have you inherited your grandfather's nose? Your great-grandmother's tenacity? Your uncle's diabetes? The stories of inheritance can even be potential careers, addictions, traits, or choices. These vibrations fill the etheric body with energetic imprints and patterns that flow through and around us, like a song we cannot get out of our heads.

Think, for a few moments, about your family stories—the ones you are proud of and those that make you cringe. Recall what you have been told, overheard, or received. Recall what you "see" with your physical eyes or with your inner eye when you look in the mirror. Do you have parts of yourself "tagged" with ancestral labels? What or whose labels are you wearing on your physical body? These tags are held within your etheric body—the energetic memory of the past. Make a list or draw a picture that illustrates what energetic imprints or ancestral inheritances you hold in the present version of yourself.

_____

_____

_____

_____

_____

_____

Attempting to label energy can be difficult. Sometimes there is physical evidence that may prove the genetic inheritance, as in physical traits. Other times, we attempt to harness abstract energies to examine them. This may be challenging. However, getting to know your etheric body is worth the effort.

As you continue to pay attention to your etheric body and the energetic memories that have come through your family stories, traits, and experiences, it is helpful to resolve any disruptive vibrations that also come through. You will help free yourself and others as you continue this important work.

Prayer for the Family Tree

The following prayerful practice can assist you in reclaiming your personal responsibility, holding your space, and healing the family tree through a practice of forgiveness:

I am, I am, I am here and now
holding space on the planet as a
co-creative being of infinite potential.
I am, I am, I am responsible for the energy I bring
to this plane.
I am sorry for all the times
I believed I was weak or powerless.

I am sorry for all the times
I blamed my ancestors, genes, family members, or God
for my experience of life.
Please forgive me.

I release my ancestors
from the misqualified energies
that have been woven
through the branches of the family tree.
I am, here and now,
recalling my energy and reclaiming my ability
to tend to the field around me.
No one else is responsible for my electromagnetic field.
I am in charge of my field.
I take back my power and my ability
to hold my space in relation to others.

I send vibrant healing light and unconditional love
through my etheric body and all
energetic imprints of past, present, future, and parallel timelines
connected to my being.
I bless and forgive my ancestors,
and I ask to be blessed and forgiven
by all future generations and aspects of myself.
And so it is.

Activation:
Dance of the Etheric Body

Dance or free movement is a terrific way to reclaim your space and energize your field. As I mentioned, dance is not just a physical movement but a connection with the etheric body, the energy field of my being. It is also rather freeing to get out of my mental/emotional capsule of judgment and explore the me that is pure energy.

1. Find a physical space where you will be undisturbed for 10 minutes.
2. Put on some music that inspires and uplifts you.
3. Stand upright, with your feet directly below you.
4. Start by breathing the air around you, feeling your lungs and the physical body, and taking in the atoms and electrons available to you.
5. Put the part of you that judges and evaluates aside. Allow your life force energy to move you in ways that are unplanned, unchoreographed, and unedited.
6. Simply allow energy to flow through you and the movements you create.
7. Remain committed to the movement exploration for at least 10 minutes or longer.

> Allow your life force energy to move you in ways that are unplanned, unchoreographed, and unedited.

Twenty Aspects of the Etheric Body

- Considering the twenty faces of the icosahedron, make a list of twenty words about this exercise and your connection to your energetic life force.
- How did this movement activate your spirit?
- Review the list of twenty words. Is there one or two that stand out to you? Perhaps a drawing, a painting, or a poem will evolve from the movement or your description of the exercise. Allow the improvisation to continue into other mediums if the inner urge calls to you.

JOURNAL
Messages from the Angels of Forgiveness

Chapter 6

The Alchemy of Apology, Forgiveness, and Ho'Oponopono

Love is the healing vibration that transcends density and raises our vibrational field. Love is an alchemical bridge that moves us from one state to another. The act of apologizing comes through the vibration of love.

Forgiveness can be a regular part of your daily cycle. Whenever there is pain that is associated with either blame, when it is tagged as someone else's cause, or shame, when it is identified as your personal failure, forgiveness is the step needed to transform the lower energies. Flowing with forgiveness can become easy and regular. This does not mean that it should not be meaningful, but like love, it should not be rare and out of reach. Forgiveness and love should be common and regular occurrences, a part of everyday life and every human interaction. Holding love for humanity, forgive easily and readily.

Some people have great difficulty when it comes to forgiveness, but some have difficulty with love, as well. A victim's mentality is as disturbing to the peace as a thief's; both do harm to the four lower bodies and need to be cleansed. Blame and shame are far more frequent companions on life's journey.

A victim mentality is as disturbing to the peace as a thief; both do harm to the four lower bodies and need to be cleansed.

B.L.A.M.E. and S.H.A.M.E.

B.L.A.M.E is an acronym for "Broken Lens and Making Excuses," while S.H.A.M.E. is "Self-Hatred and Making Excuses." With a clearer vision, we can seek the full scope of forgiveness and the energies of giving and receiving. Here are ways the need for forgiveness cycles through our lives over and over again:

Asking for God's Forgiveness

This is forgiveness for the idea of separation, which is not the truth of who we are. We have been living in a lower vibration, believing that we are separate from our Divine Presence. For this misconception, we ask for forgiveness, reconciliation, and re-connection.

Asking Someone Else for Forgiveness

I feel shame that my thought, word, or action has caused pain in the field.

Forgiving Humanity

I am releasing myself and all of humanity from the limited perceptions of life in this world. We do not have the full knowledge of the Divine Plan accessible to us in life. For our limitations, I forgive all of humanity for its ignorance and failures.

Forgiving God

I have blamed God for what has become a part of life on Earth, not realizing that my Earthly classmates and I have been co-creators on this journey as God waits for our return to oneness.

Forgiving Others

I have blamed someone else for my pain. I recall my power in this situation and release your responsibility for my energy. You are free. I am free.

Forgiving Yourself

I am feeling shame for my perceptions of inadequacy and failure. These are *my* perceptions, and they are limited and faulty. Where I have failed, I will work to do better. Where I have hurt others, I will make amends. I set myself free from unhealthy shame and other forms of ego imprisonment.

Getting stuck in pain, blame, or shame is an unconstructive use of your energy. As a living being on the earthly plane, pain is inevitable. These are simply cycles along life's journey, like the phases of the moon or the second hand on the clock. Focusing too long on any of these aspects allows it to become the lens through which you see everything else. Your focus becomes distorted, and the lens no longer shows the fullness of the world around you. Some who live their lives in blame or shame allow the broken lens to reticulate even further, so they attempt to see the world through a kaleidoscope rather than a clear lens.

> Detachment is the key to not getting "stuck" in the broken lens.

Detachment is the key to not getting "stuck" in the broken lens. Pulling the camera back further, as a film director would, provides what is called an "establishing shot." An establishing shot gives the viewer a clear perspective of the landscape. In spiritual terms, this is the practice of detachment.

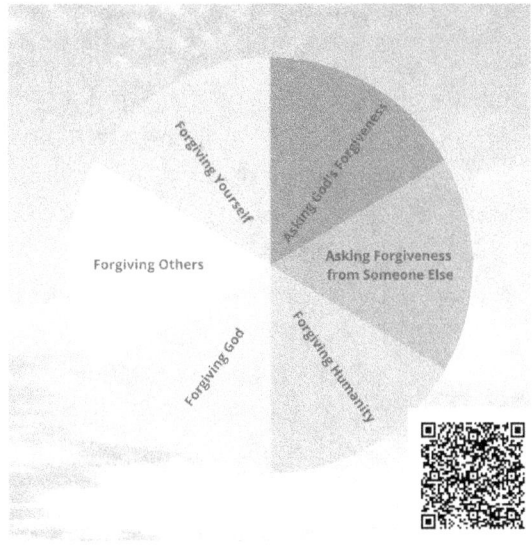

Figure 15: Wheel of forgiveness
(M. Lori Torok/Canva.com)

Activation:
Eight Breaths—The Lens of Forgiveness

1. Holding the diagram above in front of you, focus on each one of the pie slices. Take a deep cleansing breath for each one while inwardly offering loving vibrations to each area of forgiveness that may resonate within you. That will be six breaths.

2. When you have completed the six breaths, pull your visual "camera lens" back further, and see the image behind the diagram, the sky. That is your seventh breath. Send love through your breath.

3. Put the book down and breathe into what is present in the physical atmosphere around you. That is your eighth breath.

4. Feel yourself fully present in this moment, where you are safe, here and now.

5. If any part of this exercise had "sticky" energy within your thoughts or your breath, lovingly repeat the entire exercise.

Love allows us to forgive. In fact, we cannot truly forgive until we hold nothing but love for the being and the situation. Love and compassion are the light that shines through this lens. The wheel of forgiveness, above, provides a direction for love and compassion. At any given moment, we are flowing with love from one area to the next, setting everyone, including ourselves, free.

Ho'Oponopono

Ho'Oponopono is a traditional shamanic ritual from pre-contact Hawaii that has been gifted to the world through the modern and updated teachings of Mornnah Nalamaku Simeona (1913–92), who was known as a ka huna lapa'au (meaning light secret healer). At the age of seventy, in 1983, Simeona was declared a Living Treasure of Hawaii. Her organization and teachings have spread out across the globe for peaceful resolutions for millions.

Although Ho'Oponopono was traditionally conducted only among community groups and families before a **kahuna**, Simeona believed the practice could benefit humanity. In August of 1980, at the Huna World Convention, Simeona shared Ho'Oponopono, as a way of clearing personal memories that create the perception of unconstructive experiences in the outer world.

"Pono" literally means right. The word, Ho'Oponopono, means to make right more right. This form of apology is different from the Western understanding of forgiveness in that it does not place blame on anyone. Ho'Oponopono is a prayerful way of making amends to cleanse the energy between us.

We begin from a place of right, our Divine Essence of Perfection. As if to say, "As children of the Divine, you are right, and I am right. We shall call upon the Divine Presence to make the relationship more right." No one is wrong. As Simeona's practice of Ho'Oponopono is rather simple, it can be utilized by reciting the following mantra:

> *I am sorry.*
> *Please forgive me.*
> *Thank you.*
> *I love you.*

I am sorry, in this case, does not subjugate the person asking for forgiveness. This moves you out of the blame/shame construct. Instead, it is a statement of acknowledgment of the humanity of all involved. It is a recognition of the participation of life acting upon life. My memory body holds a vision of something that is/was not Divinely aligned. For that, I am sorry.

Please forgive me, for I didn't know that memory was inside me. I am asking the Divine Presence within me to assist in the release of this misqualified energy. For this, I also need to forgive myself.

Thank you, to the memories, for showing me what still needs to be cleared and healed within me and the world. Thank you to the Divine Presence for the loving assistance in freeing all concerned in this memory.

I love you is the alchemical healing energy activated in this process, and it is Divine/Higher Love that heals.

I **love you** is the alchemical healing energy activated in this process, and it is Divine/Higher Love that heals.

Ho'Oponopono Variation

As you continue to work with Ho'Oponopono, to release your need to control situations, others, and judgment, a deep trust develops. Throughout my work with the classic tradition of Ho'Oponopono, something quite remarkable began to evolve. I became aware of an energy being birthed from within the statement. I started to "feel/hear" another part being whispered after the cycle, and that is: **I am you.**

Further Guidance developed a variation of the original Ho'Oponopono to help clear the vibration of discord as you forgive someone who has brought lower frequencies into the field: I forgive you. I release you. I love you. I am you.

I am you.

Presently, I combine these two mantras into one 8-bar walking tempo mantra that brings me much peace.

I am sorry.
Please forgive me.
Thank you.
I love you.
I forgive you.
I release you.
I love you.
I am you.

Activation:
Walking Ho'oponopono

One of my favorite ways to actively practice Ho'Oponopono is to walk through the neighborhood, inwardly chanting the mantras. The short phrases offer rhythmic pulses for each step and carry me effortlessly for an hour or so without strain. First, I allow myself to focus on events resonating through my physical, etheric/memory, mental, and emotional bodies. As I recall things vibrating up, I gently hold the energy and "speak" the Ho'Oponopono phrase to the image of the person or situation. Then I will bring myself to the environment through which I walk, speaking directly to the world around me—the trees, the ground, the flowers, the clouds, the air, and so on. I will allow the chant to surround me and go where it needs to for the highest and best good of all concerned.

Activation:
Meditating with Ho'Oponopono
As a seated meditation, I use my mala beads to recite the mantra 108 times as my fingers walk over each bead, keeping track of the recitations. After going forward through the prayer beads, I will return in the opposite direction. This feels like a thorough process, as I allow my inner vision to be completely absorbed by whatever could benefit from the energetic cleansing.

As you walk or sit in meditation with Ho'Oponopono, allow your words and thoughts to cleanse the field, setting yourself and all beings free from inharmonious thoughts. Below is a list of areas I have been guided to intentionally cleanse with Ho'Oponopono:

Myself	Other individuals	Physical body
Past partners	Past teachers	Past students
Political systems	Belief systems	Institutions
Animals	Plant kingdom	Food/nourishment
Earth	Fire	Water
Air	Sound	Light
Higher Self	Spiritual Guides	Elementals
Chakra system	Home	Work
Aura/energy field	Ancestors	Future Me

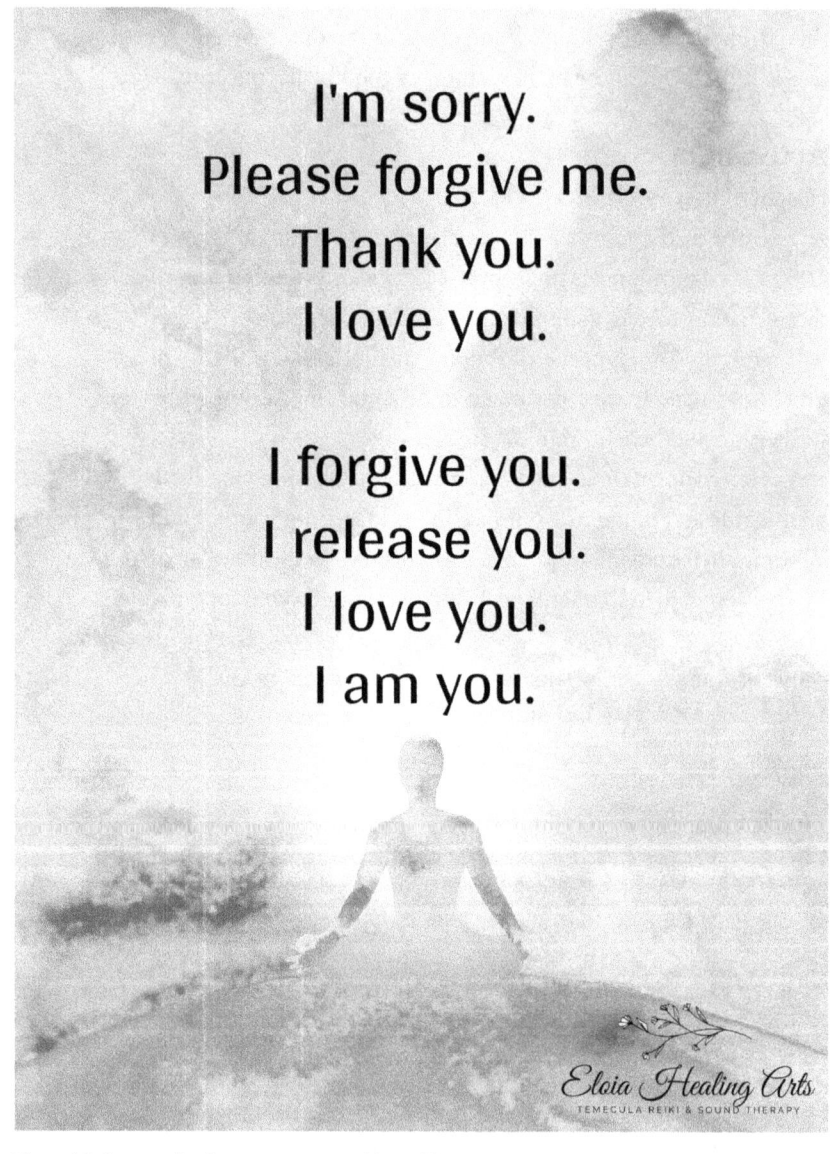

Figure 16: A prayer for forgiveness, inspired by Ho'Oponopono
(M. Lori Torok, with artwork by Benjavisa Ruangvaree/Shutterstock)

JOURNAL
Messages from the Angels of Forgiveness

Chapter 7
Reiki and Forgiveness

Accessing the etheric/memory body is truly a matter of light work. It is the interstellar, interstitial space between conscious bodies. It is beautifully cleansed and cleared in energy healing modalities, such as Reiki. Reiki is a hands-on energy healing modality that utilizes channeled **chi** or Divinely-directed universal life force energy. Anyone having difficulty clearing the energetic imprint of painful experiences may find great relief in seeing an energy healer or Reiki therapist.

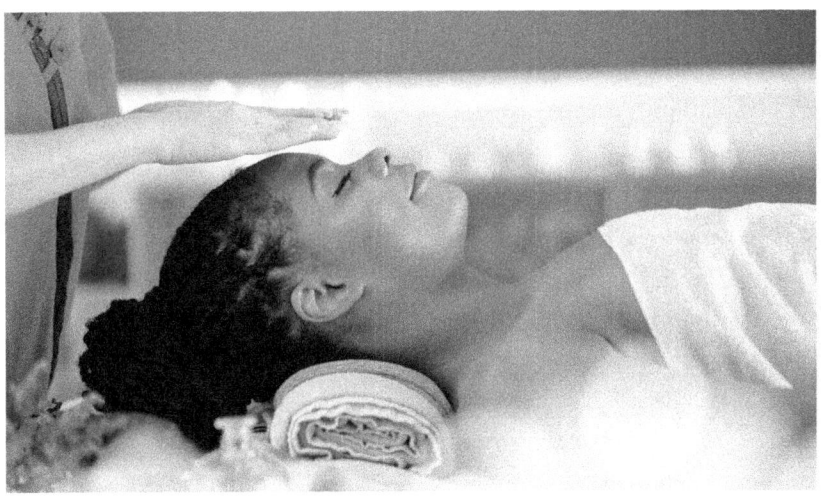

Figure 17: Image of a Reiki session (Dragon Images/Shutterstock)

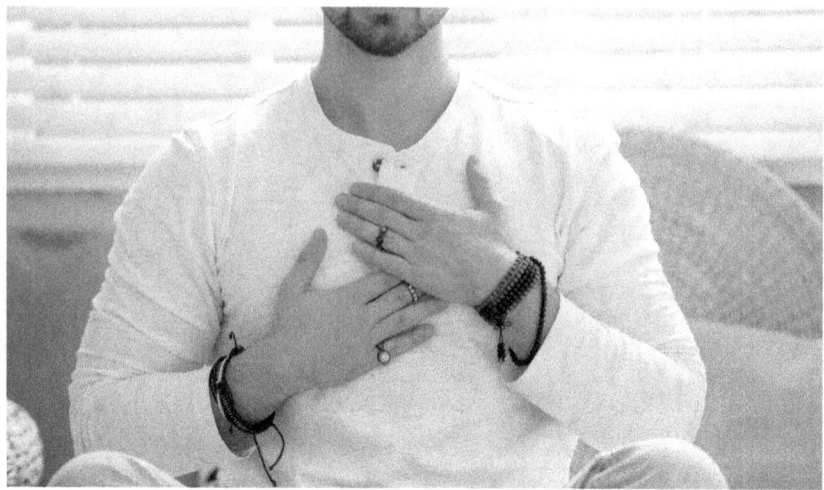

Figure 18: Image of a self-healing Reiki session (New Africa/Shutterstock)

As a **Reiki Master Teacher** and practitioner, I am happy to assist in matters of forgiveness, especially when the person can work on a deeper level than the superficial concepts of forgiveness cliches like "forgive and forget." Personally, Reiki, along with the patient guidance of the Angels of Forgiveness, has been invaluable in allowing me to clear my own painful energetic imprints of the past.

Reiki healing energy is not bound by the laws of time and space, as it is channeled from the Divine Presence, which is unlimited in potential. In the spirit world, all time is now, and all space is here. The Reiki practitioner is taught how to allow the energy to flow to the original source of the disruption. This means that wherever and whenever the disruptive energies first became an issue, the healing energy can flow to that part of the inner landscape. This is very useful in situations of generational or family tree healing. Reiki is also helpful in healing the other areas of your being, as it can heal the physical, mental, and emotional bodies affected by the etheric body.

Learning Reiki (even at just the primary class level, usually called Reiki I) can be profoundly effective for experiencing life force energy and getting a sense of its flow within your being. The Reiki student takes a class (preferably in person or at least synchronously scheduled with a live teacher holding space with the students) that is at least one full day or possibly longer. The classes I teach are at least twelve hours in length and are scheduled over two, three, or four days.

Reiki is not a practice that can be learned from a book or independently *activated*. Although many sensitive individuals have realized a strong connection to their etheric body, Reiki itself is a channeling of the energy of the Divine Presence for healing of the highest nature, not just an awareness of the energy field itself. Reiki is activated and aligned to the student's etheric body through **attunement**. Attunements, shown in figure 19, are also called placements, initiations, or empowerments. Attunements do not "give" the student the healing energy; however, it aligns the

In the spirit world, all time is now, and all space is here.

student's etheric body and chakra system to this Divine Life Force for use in healing and cleansing practices.

Reiki healing is a process by which physical, mental, emotional, and energetic blockages that accumulate in times of stress, strain, and restricted flow are released. This returns the energy field to the higher vibrations of the Divine Presence. In cases where someone has been surrounded by hurt, resentment, or anger, Reiki can release the restriction and allow the higher vibrations of light to flow freely. Sometimes just one session can release these long-held tensions. Other

Figure 19: Image of a Reiki Attunement
(Microgen/Shutterstock)

times, it gives the emotional space for the individual to begin or continue with the deep work of forgiveness, with the support of the etheric body's new freedom.

Miracles of shift and changes in perception happen regularly with Reiki. Reiki is love; God is love. There is no limitation for either. As long as the heart and mind remain open to the healing power of love, the etheric body will realign itself to the memory of Divine Consciousness held within. In the etheric body, the Divine Plan for your highest and best good remains in love and light. How wonderful that we have the gift of calling that in for our growth and healing.

Reiki Sessions for Self-Healing and Forgiveness

Someone attuned to Reiki, even just at the first level, can sit in a calm meditative state and bring Reiki to the self by placing hands over their heart, head, or any other area that feels energetically central for this deep healing work. The following statements may help you set the intention for healing and forgiveness during a self-healing Reiki session. Use all or parts of any of the following statements:

- "I ask that Reiki (Divine healing energy) move through my four lower bodies to find those places within myself where I have yet to forgive fully."
- "I ask Reiki to clear and purify my four lower bodies of all thoughts and emotions of non-forgiveness."
- "I am willing to forgive *[insert name or situation]* for all my perceived grievances."
- "If there is anything I need to know about these energies of non-forgiveness, I am willing to receive that information."
- "I am willing to learn about the time in the past (my past or past lifetimes) when these energies first became an issue for me."
- "I am willing to see this differently."
- "I forgive myself for all of my misperceptions about this world."
- "I forgive myself for all the misqualified energies I have

placed into the field."

- "I forgive the world for not being how I would have it be."
- "I forgive all who have harmed me in thoughts, words, and actions."
- "I forgive myself for harming others in my thoughts, words, and actions."
- "I forgive to be at peace."
- "I am at peace."

If there is anything I need to know about these energies of non-forgiveness, I am willing to receive that information.

The Angels of Forgiveness: A Lesson in Religions and Rainbows

A few years ago, I was assisting a friend, whom we shall call John. He was in the midst of a personal crisis. As a homosexual male in his late twenties, he had not yet come out to his family. He was concerned about their religious affiliation and how they would react. In his future vision, if he were to tell his family about his personal life, they would either need to leave the church they were completely immersed in (and had been in for generations) or disown him. This was a foreign concept to me, as I was not a part of this religious affiliation. However, my research had shown that this was not uncommon and would be a likely result of the difficult conversation that lay ahead for John and his family.

This weighed heavily on my heart. I was deeply saddened that families and institutions could be so dis-compassionate to their "own." Perhaps my four-year-old inner self, pushed out the side door in the middle of a Buffalo winter, was feeling the pangs of abandonment. Nonetheless, I found myself in meditation, asking for healing of those parts of me that were angry at John's family and church.

I heard from my Guides, the Angels of Forgiveness, "You need to forgive the Mormon Church." I was surprised, as I had no connection to the church except through conversations with John. The church had not done anything to me; why would I need to forgive them? Also, what good would it do for me to forgive a church I had no affiliation with? These questions swirled around me in a haze. Nonetheless, I knew this guidance was coming from a high vibration. Was I going to follow? Yes.

I took a deep breath and placed my Reiki hands over my heart, and sincerely stated, "I forgive the Mormon Church." Having never spoken these words before, there was an unfamiliar frequency sounding around me. I allowed the Reiki to flow, and calm settled through and around me. I acknowledged with, "Thank you."

Then I heard, "You need to forgive the Catholic Church."

"Well," I thought, "we are getting closer to home."

I grew up Catholic and felt a profound connection to this belief system until I walked out of a mass on St. Valentine's Day at St. Patrick's Cathedral in New York City in the mid-nineties when the bishop was preaching about homosexuality as a deviled expression, as anti-love. I simply stood up, turned, and walked away, knowing in my heart that speaking against love in a church could not possibly be Godly communication. Without anger or strong emotion of any kind, I simply walked away, leaving the bishop's angry voice behind me.

Since then, I had watched from a safe distance how the Catholic Church was troubled by myriads of harmful secrets and criminal improprieties. I never felt a strong judgment. But I did feel sadness and a knowing that this was not a safe place.

Nonetheless, I sat cross-legged at my meditation table, with my Reiki hands filled with light, over my heart, and followed the guidance, "I forgive the Catholic Church." Reiki moved around and through me once again. Bringing a wave of love that was even stronger than the first time. Peace.

Then, I heard the guidance once again, "Now, you must forgive all religions." This felt like an enormous hurdle as my mind flipped through volumes of religious wars, inquisitions, suppression of voices, denials, discriminations, abuses, crimes, and violations of indescribable magnitude. All beliefs, over all times. Me? Forgive? Religion? How?

I was gently guided to hold compassion for all who sought truth and belief outside themselves, for all who gave their authority away, and for all who tried to control others through fear.

With tears streaming down my face, I felt so much pain from lifetimes past, where I was caught in failures of belief systems, shining a light on religious trauma deeply entombed within me. "I forgive all religions," I said.

The next part of this story is almost too beautiful to believe, and I even hesitate to include it here because of its supernatural beauty. But if you cannot share mystical beauty, as it happens, what is the value of the experience?

While I was having this meditation/Reiki experience, my husband took our dog for a walk. On his return to the house, he told me there was a rainbow over our house. He said he saw it in the distance, but he was surprised to discover that it didn't keep moving away as he got closer, as rainbows usually do. In fact, it was directly over our home. He took this picture before coming in. A blessing.

Working with a Reiki Practitioner

Working with a professional Reiki practitioner for assistance with areas of forgiveness is a terrific way to move through the density that gets trapped in the etheric body. The energetic imprints of harsh emotions and unforgiving thoughts reverberate throughout our being and can often lead to physical patterns of weakness, illness, and dysfunction. A Reiki session can assist you in cleansing your thoughtforms as well.

The healing power of Reiki is related to the intentions you

Figure 20: Rainbow over our house, December 18, 2013
(Photo courtesy of Steve Torok and the Angels of Forgiveness)

bring to the session, so it is exceedingly helpful to set the intention that you wish to work on—areas of unforgiveness or judgment—with your practitioner. This can be done with as little or as much detail about your situation as you wish to share. It is helpful to vibrationally share some detail so you can take responsibility for your part in the disruptive energies. Sometimes, you can release what you are willing to call forth, like shining a light into the dark corners to see what is there to be cleaned out.

If you are not yet ready to discuss the details, you can also share

> Sometimes, you can release what you are willing to call forth, like shining a light into the dark corners.

that. Simply acknowledging that there are shadows that you have not yet resolved but that you would like energetic assistance in getting to where you can hold space for forgiveness can be very honest and helpful. Forgiveness can be challenging, but simply being willing to consider forgiveness in the future can get you further down the road and closer to a clear place.

Your Reiki practitioner will not force any particular outcome, and *you* set the agenda for *your* healing. A Reiki session is a sacred place where deep healing, love, and understanding are primary. Do not feel rushed or coerced in any part of the process. Being love and light, Reiki is patient and gentle in its care. That being said, Reiki can get you to the next step in your process of forgiveness as you peel away layers of blockages to get to the core of the issue.

Whether you learn Reiki or seek the assistance of a qualified Reiki professional, Divine Timing will meet you exactly where you are and gently bring you just a little, or a lot, further down the road to the clear place.

Reiki can also assist you in cleansing the field around you, so you can become more aware of the energetic influences that infiltrate your system regularly without your conscious awareness. In your work with the Divine Presence, Reiki energy, or with a qualified professional, you can learn to detach from unhealthy energies in favor of higher frequencies of Divine Light and Love.

The Wisdom of Detachment

When your energy is connected/tied to another's energy, whether by choice or even unknowingly, you are not connecting to the power of your full life force, which comes as a channel within and through you. Unwisely keeping the cords connected at the lower levels can be very draining, as you are being moved by the human/psycho-physical vibrations swirling around you.

Energy vampires are only one way your life force energy can be taken. We often willfully "give" our energy away to places and people we believe have "lost" their Divine Presence connection. This is a "charitable" donation of energy that cannot be renewed, for it is not in alignment with the flow of Divine Energy. Instead, it is an emotional cord (based on false assumptions) from one person to another. It presupposes an underlying false truth (a form of **hardwiring**) of debt consciousness: "You don't have enough, so I will give you what you don't have. I, then, need you to give it back to me when you have enough, or I'll need to get more from someone else." Or (possibly) worse, "There isn't enough for everyone, so I will horde what I have."

If you're having trouble understanding this debt-based currency (current) of energetic flow, think of how people approach their financial energy, perhaps flipping between the extremes of debt and abundance or those who remove themselves from the flow entirely to horde what they have. People will also express this in terms of love (a word that causes much distress on our vibrational plane), trying to get what *they feel* they don't have by whatever means they can.

It's Time to Set Everyone Free

Connecting only to the energetic give-and-take and horde game within your personal part of the **Flow-er of Life** is a complicated scheme. This is energetically draining, unfulfilling, and spiritually corrupt. You may feel/know it is time to set everyone free, and set yourself free in the process.

Detaching your energies from another (or from all others) is not selfish. In fact, it is an act of great love. Detachment allows everyone their Divine gift of freedom, and in the practice of detachment, you can honor the human imperative of free will.

Many times, releasing someone who has harmed us or a painful situation is part of the process of forgiveness. Parting in anger is one sure way to remain attached to others, by invisible cords that tug and pull each time they are brought to mind in the mental body. Parting requires us to remove our energetic entanglements and recall our life force energy as we move on to the next part of our journey. Releasing others is an important part of the journey to a clear place, and its work lies in the etheric body.

Detachment allows everyone their Divine gift of freedom, and in the practice of detachment, you can honor the human imperative of free will.

All detachment, for it to be effective and of a high vibration, needs to come from a place of love. Divine Love, octaves above what we currently understand love to be, is unconditional and unlimited. Detachment is an act of Divine Love; therein lies Divine Strength and Divine Wisdom.

The following invocation/prayer was given to me in **Angelic Guidance** to share with others to assist with detachment from a place of Divine Presence, Protection, and Love. This is the detachment I teach to my Reiki students and the process I undertake at the end of each of my Reiki sessions, releasing the client (or student) from the deep energetic connections of the etheric/memory body. May these forty-nine words resonate through you with the peace you seek and the joy you hold. Call forth the image of the person from whom you need to detach, and sincerely and lovingly speak these words to release you and them.

Sacred Fire Love,[12]
*Surround me with **Violet Flame**.*
Protect my light and Three-Fold Flame.[13]
Detach my energies from this cord.
Create harmony out of discord.
Raise the vibration, highest and best,
Free us from all the rest.
Bless these patterns and karmic cords.[14]
Heal the energy; centered; restored.

Activation:
Reiki for Forgiveness

Scan the QR code for an online Reiki transmission if you want some energetic help with releasing others through forgiveness. Sit or lie back and enjoy this Reiki experience, as a gift from me and the Angels of Forgiveness, to you.

After completing the 11-minute online *Reiki Session for Forgiveness*, list five to ten words to describe your experience and the thoughts/emotions that came up for you during the session.

How do you feel after this process?

Feel free to repeat this online *Reiki Session for Forgiveness* as often as you wish. The Angels of Forgiveness are happy to meet you through this work whenever you seek their assistance.

---

12 Source, Mother-Father God.

13 Three-Fold Flame: an individual's spark of Divine Presence within the secret chamber of the heart. It has three qualities, represented in three colors: pink (Divine Love), blue (Divine Strength), gold (Divine Wisdom).

14 The energetic pathway between you and another person.

JOURNAL
Messages from the Angels of Forgiveness

Chapter 8

The 4GiveNess Project

Week 2

The Temple of Truth

If you are guided to stay with the work in the sacred garden (from Week 1) a bit longer, you may want to listen to the first meditation (Week 1) once or twice more before going on to this week's meditation. Do not feel rushed to follow a calendar. Allow yourself to be inwardly guided when it is right for you to move on to the meditation below.

Meditation

This is the second meditation of The 4GiveNess Project. Scan the QR code to listen to the prerecorded audio of this guided meditation at any time.

1. Make yourself comfortable, lying down or seated, and feel free to move or shift as necessary.
2. Take a deep breath and tell your body that it is time to relax now. Know that in this space, at this time, you are

perfectly safe. Archangels are in every corner of your room for guidance and protection, for the highest and best good for all.

3. There is excitement in the air. Your Angels are thrilled that you are working on forgiving, releasing karmic burden, and setting people free for the healing good of the Earth.

4. Close your eyes. Feel yourself relax even further. With each breath, drop deeper into the core of your physical body, to your heart center. Allow yourself the release of getting out of your head space, as best you can, and moving into that Divine Heart Center, where the Three-Fold Flame burns brightly.

5. Sit inside the Three-Fold Flame, feeling the energies of Divine Strength, Divine Wisdom, and Divine Love in the heart chamber. Allow those energies to flow through your entire system.

6. In your consciousness, see mist forming around you—very much like a cloud coming around you. As you feel, see, sense, or just know that this mist is enfolding you, you begin to see that these small particles are particles of light. This light goes around you and through you—balancing you and clearing you, helping you to release any lower vibrations which may be lingering in your space.

7. As the mist finishes its job of clearing you, it dissipates, and you find yourself in your sacred garden. That beautiful garden is vibrant, lush, and full of life-force energy . . . and the colors . . . the smells . . . the sounds fill your senses, helping to clear you further and to raise your vibration.

8. As you walk through this Garden of Truth, if you see or are shown any areas that still need tending, ask for help from your Angelic Guides. Ask for guidance and support in bringing healing to the garden. Spend some time tending, in your consciousness, to the work of the garden—pruning, trimming, weeding, watering, etc. And in return, the energy of the garden heals and balances you.

9. As the work of the garden continues, you see that the colors are more vibrant and vibrating, alive with energy. The colors swirl and fill the space around you. And like the mist before, the colors now flow through you, energizing and balancing your chakras, balancing you.

10. You feel the life-force energy of the Earth beneath your feet as you connect with the beautiful Earth Star chakra, feeling it balanced and in alignment beneath you. The energy of Mother Earth/Gaia flows up through all your chakras, reaching the crown, going beyond the corona chakra, and into the Soul Star chakra—perfectly balanced, aligned, and harmonized.

11. As the colors from your chakras blend and swirl and harmonize with the colors of the garden, it is an overwhelming combination of color and light. And in this color and light, and the combining of hues, you become aware of a temple, which appears in the middle of the garden, a glowing white structure. Perhaps you saw it before, or you are seeing it now for the first time.

12. This beautiful temple in the middle of the garden is the Temple of Truth. It is white and pristine, with many stairs leading upward to a glorious doorway with pillars on both sides.

13. This temple will be accessible to those who have done a certain amount of spirit work, when you have taken responsibility for your karmic debt and realigned misqualified energies toward light and love. It will not be accessible to all at this point. But not to worry, you are on the path, and you will continue to be guided and led when the timing is right for you.

14. This temple is the heart of the garden. The garden represents the outer body. You may be asked to remain in the outer garden for a while as you continue to work with the healing energies of the plants, flowers, and trees. Remember to ask forgiveness and understanding of the

thoughts and actions which have precipitated outward through your channel. If this is the case, you are asked to smile through your spirit and go further into the garden experience and ask for release, grace, and forgiveness. The life energies around you will be there to assist.

15. You may be guided to pause here.

16. If the inner urgings of your heart lead you to enter the temple, proceed up the immense stairway, with the Angels of Forgiveness, with your Guide, who will lead you forward to open the door for you.

17. This is the Temple of Truth. See, feel, sense, and know the energies of this magnificent Divine Space.

18. This is a place of balance where the energies of truth and comfort complement each other. It is an understanding of truth that will assist you on your Divine Path toward illumination, enlightenment, and ascension.

19. In this magnificent retreat, you will feel the vibration of the momentum of truth on all sides of your being.

20. This Divine Vibration will move through you to shift misqualified or misdirected energies. The light held within this temple disperses the shadows of your consciousness.

21. Repeat for yourself: "The light held within this temple disperses the shadows of my consciousness."

22. Use your attention/focus to invoke the vibration of truth, allowing the shadows of human concepts to dissolve from your consciousness, releasing old inharmonious vibrations from your screen of life.

23. Allow time to move forward unhurriedly during this inner work

24. In this temple, you may be aware of beautiful Ascended Masters/Teachers and Angelic Presences serving to help those coming here for healing of their human physical forms. The Angels and Masters embody truth. It is impersonal. Truth is based on the Laws of Life. You, too, may begin to feel the vastness of these concepts. The more

you visit this sacred temple, the clearer you will become—the more you can assist in anchoring truth, releasing the need for fluctuating opinions, false descriptions, judgment, anger, and disharmony.

25. Truth is impersonal, based on the Laws of Life.

26. In this pristine sacred temple dedicated to the virtue of truth, humbly ask your Higher Self to initiate an attunement sequence of self-forgiveness for our own lack of understanding of truth.

27. The veil of human forgetting had been placed around you, and it is now being released, allowing you to re-member the truth of Divine Will, the truth of the Laws of Life.

28. To proceed on your path, to assist in the healing of the Earth, you must forgive yourself for all ways you participated in the lower vibrations of false pretense. Ask for assistance in allowing you to forgive yourself for all the ways you participated in the lower vibrations of false pretense, in this life and in every other lifetime.

29. In this Temple of Truth, you can forgive yourself for what you participated in that was not truth. And in this light, in this vibration, it is dissolved. Do not carry it forward; do not bring that misqualified vibration with you. Let it go here. Allow the release. The light dissolves the shadow, and it lingers no longer. The light dissolves all shadows, and they linger no longer. Truth sets you free.

30. The truth of who you are is held in this Divine Space—the Temple of Truth. Hold that frequency around you now. Truth.

31. With gratitude, take a deep breath of truth, and let it vibrate through you, through the physical body.

32. Bring awareness back to your physical body in the physical space, pulling your consciousness down to the Earth Star chakra beneath your feet.

33. Feeling the vibrancy of your own life force energy, bring awareness to the area behind your eyes. As you gently

The light dissolves all shadows, and they linger no longer. Truth sets you free.

blink your eyes, see the world of matter around you, as if for the first time—seeing all the shapes, colors, light, and shadows. Be fully present, here and now. Awaken.

Meditation Response

Describe your experience of the mist and light particles at the beginning of the experience. What did you see/hear/feel? Was there anything, in particular, that felt important about the experience of the clearing activity of these particles?

How did the garden look to you today? Was it different from your previous experiences? Do the changes in its appearance have any significance to you?

What did you do in the garden today? What was brought to your attention? Did you receive a message about the appearance/activity in the Garden? What do you want to remember about your work in the garden? Is there work still to be done there?

If you moved into the Temple of Truth, what was your experience of the attunement sequence of self-forgiveness? What do you want to remember about the truth of who you are?

Activations:
Living in the Truth

After completing the meditation for Week 2, the activations below will assist you on the journey of forgiveness.

1. Spend time this week meditating on/journaling how you process information/energy around you. So much of what we receive through our senses is not the truth, but opinions, ideas, perspectives, and, most certainly, conditioning. Truth is unconditional, unwavering, and constant. It is time to exercise your ability to discern the energy frequencies around you. Daily, make a note of those times that you are aware of your own perceptions and opinions masquerading as truth. What do you observe? How do those observations feel?

2. In the moment, when in conversation or hearing/reading news headlines, pondering the past, or making plans for the future, check in with your **solar plexus chakra** (which connects us to the creative energies of the Great Sun) to feel if the information being presented to you or perceived by you is TRUTH. Try to do this every day for a week, at random times throughout your day.
   - When you feel/find an idea that doesn't resonate with Divine Truth, do not judge or react from a place of anger/frustration/disappointment. Instead, ask your Angels/Teachers to show you the truth and see/feel/hear/sense where your thoughts go next. There is much available to you in this process. But the important key is to ask to be shown the TRUTH.
   - Notice how the vibration of truth resonates within you and raises the energy out of the level of the solar plexus (emotions) and into the heart (love).
   - Continue to connect, reach up, and work with your own Angels/Teachers as they are always with you. If you presently feel a disconnect with your Angelic team of Guides, there are particular Angels/Ascended Masters/

Forgiveness: Journey to a clear place

Teachers most readily able to assist you in connecting with truth in the process and action of forgiveness. Simply call the Angels of Forgiveness or the Angels of the Fourth Ray, the ray of truth and healing, and they will gladly answer your every call for assistance.

Blessings to your journey!

JOURNAL
Messages from the Angels of Forgiveness

PART III

The Physical Body:
The Elements and
the Elementals

Figure 21: Icosahedron (Photo: Anne Watson)

Chapter 9

Sacred Fire

Fire, in the system of the Platonic solids, is represented by the three-dimensional shape of the pyramid. It holds the metaphysical property of protection and is aligned with the cardinal direction of the South.

Understanding the circumstances of the harmful experience is the first step to forgiveness and, ultimately, healing. This happened. You were hurt or harmed in some way. You had this experience. You must hear the story, feel the pain, and own the truth. As much as this **lifestream** can be called reality, it was/is real to you and in you. As you re-member the painful experience, you make it a living reality within your energy field, as if it were happening to you in the present moment. Childre and Martin, in their insightful work, *The Heartmath Solution,* state that because our emotional history and reactions can be triggered unconsciously and then bypass the mind's reasoning process, it takes a power stronger than the mind to change emotional patterning.[15]

Figure 22: The element of fire, as represented in the Platonic solid pyramid. (Magic Pictures/Shutterstock)

You must hear the story, feel the pain, and own the truth.

---

15 Childre, Doc & Martin, Howard. (2011). *The Heartmath Solution.* HarperOne, New York. P. 142.

The Invitation of the Mystic

The mystical power stronger than our mind is the Divine Presence; you may call it the Divine Creative Principle, Creator, Source, Spirit, or God. Specifically, working with the **Great Rays** of Divine Light, you can harmonize the four lower bodies to get clear and raise your vibrational frequency. The mystic is guided by the truth of the inner connection with the Divine Spirit. This is a path available to everyone who makes an effort of clearing their energy field and raising their vibration, even a modicum, so that the Divine Spirit is invited to bridge the gap created by the human lens and belief in separation.

The mystic moves beyond and through this separation to get through the veil which never existed. The mystic becomes a channel and ally of Divine Guidance, activating the Divine Presence within the heart center. The heart center is a portal to the higher octaves, which brings the connection of the Divine into the here and now, confirming that there was never any separation of time or space. All time is now, and all space is here, for we are One. With that, there is no real journey of distance or time; there is no path. The mystical connection to God is here and now. God is always available to you, just as you are available to you. No need to travel to find the God you seek; look within, dear one.

No need to travel to find the God you seek; look within, dear one.

As sons and daughters of human parents, we are experiencing the physical world through a physical body, operating under the laws of physics. The forces operating in this physical experience have been organized into life forces called elements. There are Divine Energies inherent in these elements, as well.

Let's examine the word, *element*. "El" is the name of the Canaanite God in the Hebrew Bible. "Ment" is a suffix that makes the preceding noun concrete due to an action or quality. Together, the word element literally becomes "God in action."

The classical world identified four elements, or life forces, operating on all levels of being: fire, air, earth, and water. My mystical connection has identified and requested that I work with a fifth element: sound. Each of these offers a unique opportunity for the traveler on the path of forgiveness to support the journey.

Sacred Fire Energy

The elementals of fire, the salamanders, and beings of the **lizard kingdom** carry the energy of protection for humanity. In our own physical world, fire can be quite destructive and hold much fear for us, just as these beings of the lizard kingdom may hold fearful responses for the individual, as well. The beautiful beings of the lizard kingdom (snakes, crocodiles, even the mystical fire-breathing dragon) have taught me not to fear their presence, for they bring great light and protection to humanity. It is our own image and discomfort that have made these powerful and protective spirits a fearful sight to many. And so it is with fire.

The truth behind the energy of sacred fire is that it is a transformative energy, which alchemizes lower energies into higher vibrations, bringing the lower density into the higher energies of spirit. This extraordinary healing power is offered to us for those who can connect with and utilize its energies for the higher good.

Fire is the energy associated with the solar plexus chakra, being of the sun and the energy of human emotion. No wonder there is such fear for many locked within fire energy. Bringing calm to our own emotions can be the very protection we need. Do not underestimate the healing that you need in the areas of your own emotions and your subconscious response to fire, and fear, in general.

One day, while deep in my meditation practice, I asked what it meant to truly forgive, to release the energy attached to unresolved hurt truly, and to finally forgive completely. Although I had asked this question many times, I felt an inner urgency bordering on insistence. The inner voice of my Higher Angels spoke gently and assuredly to me as they told me to put two pieces of selenite in my hands (more about selenite a bit later). I picked up two long sticks of selenite, one in each hand, and was told to raise them high above my head. My arms formed something like a V-shape overhead. I saw/felt/knew with my inner eye that the selenite was

> Fire is the energy associated with the solar plexus chakra, being of the sun and the energy of human emotion.

suddenly "lit" with a burning Pink Flame of spiritual energy. This was not in the physical, but it was much more powerful. I was told this Pink Flame held the vibration of Divine Love and to bring this flame around me, to burn the residue of the non-loving energies around and through me. I brought the selenite torches crossed in front of me and circled the sticks around my sides and back up over my head—as if I were taking off a garment over my head. I felt radiation moving through my body. I repeated this twice more and felt clearer with each pass. I heard that I was to "set myself on fire" to release feelings of pain and non-forgiveness. I felt a deep shift in my energy, and I was exceedingly grateful for this sort of fire blessing as I went about my day.

Not really thinking much more about this beautiful experience, I attended a theatrical dance concert later the same day. I was in the audience enjoying beautiful dance and artistry when a piece began, and the musical accompaniment started to disturb me. I'm not sure what it was in particular, but the tones and qualities of the music felt like it was strangely burrowing into me. My inner voice of guidance told me to close my eyes. Immediately I saw myself performing—as if in a film—to this music. I was holding two very large torches lit with Pink Flame. My inner dance led me down a long hallway lined with people and events from various times in my life, across all times of my life, it seemed. I was running/dancing down this hallway, setting it all on fire with the Pink Flame of Divine Love. This continued throughout the rest of the dance piece and concluded exactly when the music ended. The applause began, and I was "brought back" to my seat in the theatre. Gratitude. This was the start of my journey with sacred fire.

I am told that this process of "setting yourself on fire" will work for everyone who wants to reduce the dysfunctional energies surrounding them. One of the beautiful outcomes of working with fire is that the energy isn't indiscriminately sent out into the field to disturb others within the Flow-er of Life. Fire doesn't move energy out or down the road (like water and air). Instead, it transmutes the energy, raising it. This vibrational rising is what we all need from time to time, if not daily. You cannot do this work too often.

The Color of the Flame

Different qualities are inherent in the various frequencies of color; this is mostly related to the qualities of the **Great Rays.** Below is a short list of the color frequencies which may be helpful for you in working with the element of fire in forgiveness:

Pink - Divine Love

Violet - Transmutation

Gold - Wisdom

Green - Truth and healing

Blue - Strength and protection

White - Purity

The Violet Flame

The Violet Flame is a sacred gift given to humanity through the generous Divine Energies of the 7th Ray and its **Elohim**: Arcturus and Victoria. This was delivered to us through the love and guidance of Ascended Master St. Germain, the sponsor of humanity in the Aquarian Age. Calling in the Violet Flame for Divine Assistance and the upliftment of lower energies is a great service. This may be used for forgiveness and transformation of all anti-love energies, no matter where they make themselves known. **Lightworkers** are asked to call in the Violet Flame to surround the planet daily to transmute humanity's lower vibrations.

Lightworkers are asked to call in the Violet Flame to surround the planet daily to transmute humanity's lower vibrations.

I am shown that the gem/crystal amethyst holds the vibration of the Violet Flame. Having one near or on your person may be of assistance if you are working to transmute energies and raise vibrations.

> *"The action of the Sacred Fire is much like the action of the Phoenix. Burn to be reborn, anew, free—released of the karmic burden of this Human Cycle—a resurrection of the Soul."[16]*

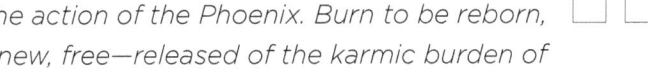

16 I receied this teaching in meditation from the Angels of Forgiveness.

Activation:
Fire of Forgiveness

As you follow this meditation, set the intention to allow room for your inner guidance and Angels to work with you.

1. Find a place where you will be undisturbed for a while. Perhaps, bring an amethyst into your room with you, or place it near you during this meditation. Light a candle to create a sacred space.

2. Sit comfortably, facing south (the cardinal direction of the element of fire), if you can. Place your hands in your lap in the Rudra Mudra (index and fourth fingers pressed down by the thumb on each hand). Alternatively, hold two sticks of selenite.

3. Bring your awareness to the solar plexus energy center (Manipura chakra) in the area of the abdomen above your naval. Breathe into the solar plexus, as air is fuel for fire. Notice what comes forward for you in your physical sensations, your inner vision, and/or your emotions.

4. Allow the fire energy from your abdomen to expand into your field until it surrounds you on all sides, below you, and reaches up above you. What color is your fire? If you cannot "see" the color of the fire with your inner eye, ask your beautiful Angels to tell you what color it is and anything else you need to know about this fire and what it is clearing from your four lower bodies.

5. Sit in this transformative fire of forgiveness for as long as you feel guided.

6. When you return from your meditation, pull your consciousness back in, down to your feet, to the Earth Star chakra below you. Feel balanced on this southern axis and fully connected to your physical form.

7. Note your thoughts and feelings about your experience during this meditation.

....

....

What color was your fire of forgiveness? What thoughts and images appeared in your inner vision or in a more abstract sense?

....

....

....

....

How do you feel now, after coming out of the fire?

....

....

....

....

Is this a meditation you want to do again, at another time? What will you do differently? How will you change your approach to this meditation?

....

....

....

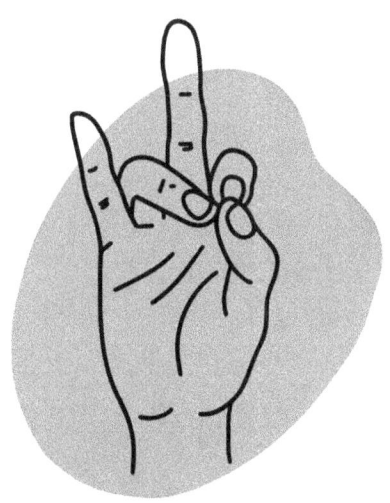

Figure 23: Rudra Mudra, a hand gesture associated with the opening of the Solar Plexus chakra/Manipura, the fire center in the area above the navel (D. Things/Shutterstock)

JOURNAL
Messages from the Angels of Forgiveness

Chapter 10

Sacred Air

Air, according to the system of the Platonic solids, is represented by the octahedron and is aligned with the metaphysical energies of communication and the cardinal direction of the East. The elementals of sacred air are the sylphs, fairies, and wisps, the feathered beings of light.

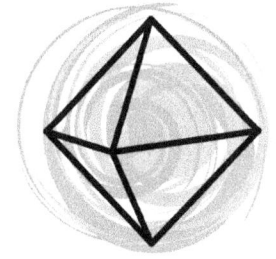

Figure 24: The element of air as represented in the Platonic solid octahedron. (Magic Pictures/Shutterstock)

Breathing is a basic life function that is primarily a subconscious activity. We take in the air around us 24 hours a day; that's around 20,000 breaths, for each living person, for every rotation of the Earth. An alchemical transformation occurs within the body as we breathe. Nitrogen, oxygen, water, carbon dioxide, ozone, and other compounds are created naturally as a result of human activity. We are engaged in an alchemical process that transmutes energy.

My Angels have told me: We are not just alchemists; we are alchemy. They have explained that the flow of energy and its transformations happen because of us, through us, with every breath exchange we take. Like most things in life, it is too simplistic to think that breathing is for our own sake only. There is a giving to the receiving in all energy, as with breathing. We give,

We co-create the world by breathing life into life, by speaking worlds into existence.

we receive; we receive, we give. Inhale; exhale. Inhale; exhale. And so it is. We co-create the world by breathing life into life, by speaking worlds into existence.

Calling In Energy with the Air

When we inhale, we attract, call in, and pull in all the energy of the air around us. This air is filled with atoms and molecules—the building blocks of all elements. The atoms are surrounded by orbiting electrons—the creative breath of the Divine, connected to the Great Rays. The electrons are microcosms of the Divine Presence, ready to activate our thoughts and e-motions (energy in motion) into the world of matter.

While the air is in the lungs, surrounding the heart's flame, the electrons are charged/qualified with our intention, the energy that we hold moment-by-moment, whatever that may be—love, kindness, disappointment, anxiety, etc. With the new quality attached to these electrons of creative impulse, we exhale that energy into the field. It moves into the field around you, and as you now know, it informs the fields of those around you.

Further still, that requalified energy of the electron stabilizes itself into the world of matter, into Mother Earth. And so we create 20,000 times a day, every day. We create from our thoughts and our emotions through the air we breathe. We hold the creative power of breath to create a world of beauty and peace. The electronic essence of air becomes our life and energetic canvas upon which we paint worlds.

The electronic essence of air becomes our life and energetic canvas upon which we paint worlds.

Activation:

"I Am" Clearing the Air

It may be beneficial for you to review the Activation in Chapter 1, Squaring the Breath at this time.

The breathing activation, below, establishes your mindful use of the electronic essence surrounding you in collaboration with the Divine Presence within. This intentional breathing exercise will energize the field around you while calming the physical body and mind.

1. Holding your left hand over the solar plexus chakra and the right hand at the level of the chest, in front of you, with your palm facing outward. For this exercise, the left hand receives the light of the solar plexus (inhale), and the right hand is giving expression out into the field (exhale).
2. Set a high-vibrational intention, like love, peace, kindness, or forgiveness.
3. Inhale the electronic essence (air) that surrounds you. Fill the lungs deeply, expanding the lower ribs at the level of the diaphragm. The shoulders and neck should remain relaxed without tensing or lifting.
4. Exhale percussively by contracting the diaphragm sharply, with a quick exhale followed by a slightly longer beat. The mouth will be open, and the sound will be "Ha." This exhalation will be similar to the heart-beat pattern of &1, &2, &3, &4. (ba-dum, ba-dum, ba-dum, ba-dum). Feel this heartbeat as the sound of "I AM."

Rhythm:	&1	&2	&3	&4
Sound:	ha, ha	ha, ha	ha, ha	ha, ha
Intention:	I Am	I Am	I Am	I Am

5. Try to exhale for four at least "heartbeats." More would be lovely (&5, &6, etc.). Don't fret if you can only exhale two or three "ha's"/ "I am's"
6. Repeat the inhale and percussive exhale for at least four cycles or as long as you feel comfortable.
7. The final breath will be one long exhale of "Ha." This final Ha-breath empties the lungs fully, pouring your Divine creative energy into the field. The inner intention is the statement, "I am the Divine presence in action."
8. Show gratitude to the air you breathe.
9. Close your eyes and feel the upliftment and strength circulating within and around you.

In the space below or in your journal, note the high-vibrational intention you created for this activation.

....

....

....

What thoughts or images came up for you as you called to your **"I Am" presence** on the percussive exhale?

....

....

....

When it came to the final long "Ha-breath," what shifts or changes did you feel?

....

....

....

You can explore this breathing exercise consecutively for a few days, using different high-vibrational intentions each time. This activation is particularly helpful when you are feeling foggy or in a low-energy state. This is both revitalizing and calming, as it brings you back into alignment with your I am presence and the creative use of the electronic essence of air.

The Forgiving Thoughtform

The element of air is aligned with the body's energy center (chakra) of the heart. It is through the heart center that the forgiving thoughtform is extended around the self and around any situation with which you find difficulty in holding in peace.

Opening the door of the heart allows the energy to expand to fill your inner space, moving outward in concentric circles, like rings around a planet, emanating from your heart. See, feel, sense, or just know the energies moving through and around you on the physical plane. The first color ring is pink, the loving core of who you are in Divine Creation. The second color ring, which surrounds the pink circle, is gold, the Divine Wisdom within. The third color ring, which surrounds the gold, is blue, connecting with Divine Strength. The outer color surrounding them all is violet, the transmutation of lower energies, no matter where they came from.

Opening the door of the heart allows the energy to expand to fill your inner space, moving outward in concentric circles, like rings around a planet, emanating from your heart.

You may call this energy in to surround you whenever you need to bring forward the thoughts of forgiveness. Concretizing the thought with this physical representation is helpful and highly effective. Even if it feels like an exercise of the imagination, at first, get comfortable seeing yourself within the colored rings of the forgiving thoughtform: pink, gold, blue, violet/purple.

You may also call in the forgiving thoughtform around anyone you wish to forgive but are having difficulty getting to that point. See both of you surrounded by rings or spheres of these colored energies—with pink (love being at the core of both of you). Envision both of you standing next to each other, with the forgiving thoughtform overlapping in a shared space and the immaculate concept, within the Flow-er of Life, in the peace of the forgiving thoughtform.

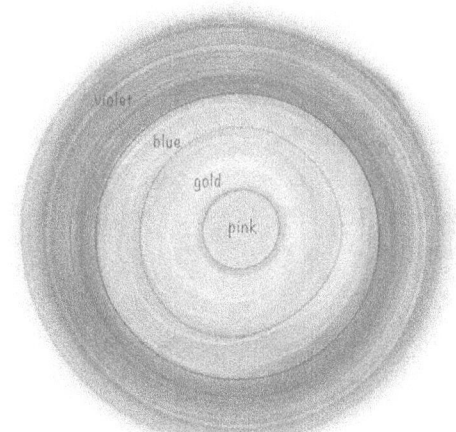

Figure 25: The Forgiving Thoughtform (M. Lori Torok)

Activation:
The Forgiving Thoughtform

1. Think of someone in your life or in the world spotlight whom you have difficulty understanding or forgiving. To start, choose just one person—later, you can choose groups of people or even situations, systems, or institutions. Take a moment to ask yourself, on a scale of one to ten, what level of discomfort is brought forward when you think of this person and the issue you have trouble forgiving. Note the number.

2. Close your eyes and bring in the image/feeling of the forgiving thoughtform around you. Pink in the center, throughout your body's physical form, and out into your energy field. Surround that with golden light; surround that with blue light; surround that with violet light.

3. Now bring the other person next to you in your consciousness. Holding the circles or spheres of light around you, do the same for them. Pink in the center, surrounded by gold, surrounded by blue, and finally surrounded by violet.

4. See, in your mind's eye, how both of your circles overlap. Allow the forgiving thoughtform to do its sacred work. There is no need for you to direct or control this activation; simply allow.

5. Remain in this space for a few moments (5–10 minutes). Notice what you notice. What thoughts arise? What feelings come to the surface? Just notice. Note how you feel now about this person and the piece that has been challenging to forgive.

6. On a scale of one to ten, what level of discomfort is brought forward for you now when you think of this person and the issue you have trouble forgiving? Note the number.

7. Release the process in gratitude.

Allow the forgiving thoughtform to do its sacred work.

In the space below or in your journal, create an artistic response to your experience of the forgiving thoughtform. This may be a dialogue, a poem, a list of words, a drawing, a painting, or something altogether different to represent your experience with the forgiving thoughtform.

JOURNAL
Messages from the Angels of Forgiveness

Chapter 11

Sacred Earth

Working with the healing energies of Mother Earth/Gaia/Sophia provides us with endless opportunities for grounding and a deeper understanding of our experiences in this lifestream. In the Platonic solids, Earth energy is represented by the cube and is aligned to the cardinal direction of the North. The elementals of the Earth are the nature devas who alight every plant kingdom lifeform.

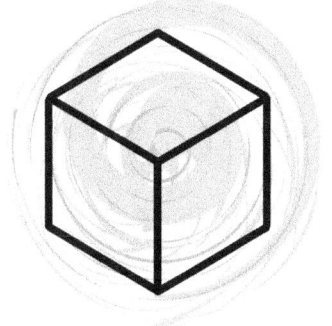

Figure 26: The element of earth as represented in the Platonic solid cube. (Magic Pictures/Shutterstock)

Many well-intentioned students/clients come to my Center to learn about meditation practices. When I speak about "grounding," a glaze comes over their faces as they disconnect from the concept. There is a common fallacy about grounding and what it is. Many are taught to "ground" by placing something like cords or roots from their physical being into the earth. They are taught to "root" into the earth. For many, this is problematic, as they subconsciously resist being planted or stuck in one place. In fact, many hold a not-so-secret desire to fly. Why do we tell them they need to be stuck on the earth?

I resisted this for many years until I was guided by Spirit that I had misunderstood the image/intention. Instead, I was

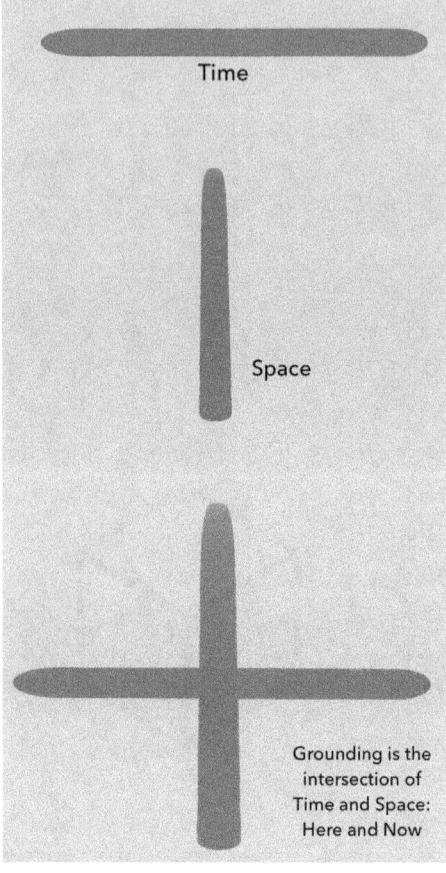

Figure 27: Grounding as the intersection of space and time, or here and now (M. Lori Torok)

told to think of grounding as connecting to the here and now. The horizontal line is often how we picture time on the Earthly plane—past, present, and future being dots on the horizontal line as if we were traveling a path from left to right, onward through time. The vertical line represents our sense of space, through us, in this lifestream. I was told to stop thinking about grounding as "getting stuck" in the earth but instead to bring the horizontal and the vertical together, bringing all time into the now and all space into the here. This is also a terrific process for pulling your energies back into your being if you have been "giving away" your life force in multiple directions. These perpendicular lay lines do not merely float above the ground.

Stop thinking about grounding as "getting stuck" in the earth. Bring the horizontal and the vertical together, bringing all time into the now and all space into the here.

The Earth Star Chakra and Your Thoughts

We are centered on and connected to the life force energy of Mother Earth through the Earth Star chakra, and it freely moves with us, just as all of the chakras do, wherever they are located within the **kinesphere.**

The Earth Star chakra will sometimes shift beneath us. After assisting hundreds of clients to locate and return the Earth Star chakra to its proper place, as the southern axis, directly between the feet, I have learned that it responds to our thoughts and emotions. When someone is particularly stressed or overcome by anxiety, fear, or uncertainty, the Earth Star chakra will take that as a sign that 1. You are under energetic attack, or 2. That you are deciding not to use the assistance that Mother Earth can provide. Because of your inherent right to the freedom of your will (free will), the Earth Star chakra will release you from its energy. Subsequently, your entire chakra system responds in kind. The chakras "close down" for self-protection, per your thoughtform.

Depending on the amount of stress you have experienced, how you have dealt with that stress, and your spiritual connection, this withdrawal from the energetic support of the Earth Star chakra may be chronic. Everyone should understand that the same system that caused it to shift and move out of its designated placement can also bring it back: your thought.

Simply breathe into that space between your feet (about 24 inches/61 centimeters below the feet). See, feel, sense, or just guess where that chakra is now, with kind appreciation—gratitude for its essential work—ask it to move back into place, or nudge it there, now, using your mind. It *will* follow your thoughts and feelings. Connect and realign. Notice how you feel now. Breathing easier? A bit of tension falling away, perhaps from your abdomen? Your brow? What else do you feel?

We have become quite accustomed to living without the energy of our chakras flowing healthily, gripping, forcing, pushing onward, with a body that feels like bricks. Sometimes emergent situations arise where we all need to work from places like this, in a world like this. However, many stay in the emergency energy far too often, for too long. This is not ideal. I recommend connecting with the Earth Star chakra several times a day, particularly as stressful thoughts or feelings arise throughout the day.

With mindful attention to the Earth Star chakra, you will find your connection to the "new normal" quickly and efficiently. After that, any disruption will be recognized early and remedied very quickly. This process is transformative for many. It is the first step to your holding space amid chaotic energies.

Working with Crystals, Minerals, and Gems

The Earth gives us everything we need to heal, as we are made of the same minerals on our planet. There is a reason why crystals and gemstones catch our eye as beautiful expressions of love from one to another. And so it is with the expression of forgiveness.

The Earth gives us everything we need to heal, as we are made of the same minerals on our planet.

Several crystals and minerals are recommended for assisting with the difficulties of forgiveness in all its forms—giving and receiving. Holding the piece in your hand or placing it somewhere on your person can be very helpful in entraining to the vibrational frequency and qualities of the gem.

Clearing your crystals, minerals, and gems can be significant, as (like people) they may pick up energies from other sources, which may affect their clarity and frequency.

There are many ways to "clear" your crystals. One of my favorites is to use selenite, named after the Greek moon goddess Selene (Roman equivalent: Luna). Selenite is a crystalline form of gypsum found under the desert. When the desert was an ocean floor millions of years ago, water was trapped beneath the sandy surface. When it evaporated, it formed crystal structures made almost entirely of sea salt and calcium, along with the vibrational healing energies of water and earth. Placing selenite with your other crystals will ensure a continual clearing of the **energetic field**. Selenite itself never needs clearing. It is a welcomed addition to all energy work. Selenite is the mineral described earlier (see chapter 9), when I was shown to use fire to clear the energies of the past.

Below is a list of other pieces from the mineral kingdom that may assist you with the specific work of forgiveness. They have helped many of my students and clients over the years, as I have called upon these lovely earth helpers regularly.

Rose Quartz

This beautiful, gentle stone of love is found worldwide and comes in colorations from strong light pink to soft golden white. Rose quartz is associated with the energies of compassion and mercy and the blessings of Guanyin/Kuan Yin. Rose quartz is uplifting and heart-healing, bringing all peace and love. It can provide the heart-opening (although it can energize each chakra) required to heal the areas of non-loving thoughts and feelings. Rose quartz is often associated with the energies of the **3rd Ray** and brings the mindful seeker closer to the healing energies of Heros and Amora, Ascended Master Paul the Venetian, and Archangel Chamuel and Archaea Charity.

Amethyst

This quartz has varying degrees of manganese and iron, which produces coloration that ranges from the deepest purple to the lightest lavender. Amethyst holds the transmutable potential of the Violet Flame, as mentioned above, and can help calm the pain of separation within the self—even for those pieces of loss. This is a stone of integration with the Higher/Ascended Self, as it raises the vibrational field all around. Amethyst connects the mindful seeker with the **7th Ray** and the energies of Arcturus and Victoria, St. Germain, Lady Ascended Master Portia, Archangel Zadkiel, and Archaea Amethyst. Each of them is most welcoming of your calls for assistance with the process of forgiveness.

Diopside

This lovely earth helper is found chiefly in China, India, Siberia, and the US. I am shown to use this when there is a need to open the pathway, from the heart, as an opening to the portal of forgiveness. This is particularly helpful when there has been physical trauma or emotional scars from oppositional energy, which has not been resolved in the heart center. Diopside can help people ground to the Earth Star chakra to strengthen their relationship with Mother Earth. For that reason, Diopside can also help heal unresolved issues with mother figures in your life. Diopside can be found in many different colors and shades; for the work of forgiveness, green diopside may be most helpful.

Fuschite/Green Muscovite

This powerful master healer assists with issues surrounding forgiveness, notably if the one who has been hurt and somehow accepted this pain as his role in this life or within the family/circle. Often this is described as a "martyr" type acquiescence into self-pity. This piece can be beneficial in healing as one starts to uncover/re-discover the power of his own free will in his relationships and with the outer world.

Gold

Gold, in all its color variations, is a terrific healing element that encourages strength and higher connection. In the work of forgiveness, Gold can assist in diminishing the ego, which often challenges those seeking to get past the perception of hurt. In Melody's *Love is in the Earth,* she states that Gold symbolizes the purity of the spiritual aspect of "All That Is. It is symbolic of spirituality and development in complete understanding, allowing one to attain and maintain communion with the source of all being."[17]

Archaean Butterstone

This ancient mineral dates back over 2.5 billion years, and I am called to bring this piece in the help with energies of disparity. The frequency of this stone can assist one in connecting with her true function on earth and her higher, more profound connection to life. It helps her get out of her own way, if she is ready, to see the truth of her function. Forgiveness is often the key to that function in this lifetime. This stone is considered rare, but it will be helpful for your karmic journey, which takes you through forgiveness and beyond.

This is a short list of energetic helpers from Mother Earth to assist with healing issues with forgiveness. Indeed, many others

---

17 Melody. (1995). *Love is in the Earth.* Earth-Love Publishing, US. P. 298.

can help, depending on your personal resistance and blocks to the process of forgiveness.

Once you have chosen a particular crystal, mineral, or gem, bring it into meditations with you, perhaps programming it to hold the highest vibrations of loving kindness, to hold your hand through the doors of forgiveness. Sometimes, just knowing you have this energetic support in your hand (or pocket), you can open the doors of the heart—which always open from the inside—to allow what needs to move forward, releasing the energies of the past. This can be done in a holy instant of grace without much preparation or delay. May the healing energies of love abundantly flow for you with ease.

Forgiveness and Essential Oils

Forgiveness

Forgiveness is the fragrance, rare and sweet,
That flowers yield when trampled on by feet
That reckless tread the tender, teeming earth;
For blossoms crushed and bleeding yet give birth
To pardon's perfume; from the stern decrees
Of unforgiveness. Nature ever flees.[18]

Essential oils are volatile (evaporative) liquids distilled from plants whose compounds, aromas, and frequencies have been used throughout human history. Going back to ancient Vedic literature (*c.* 1500–1200 BCE), hundreds of substances were used for liturgical and therapeutic purposes. From early folkloric medicines, traditional sacred ceremonies, and native cultures, man has utilized plants for healing, transformational and sacred purposes. Mother Earth has provided us with countless ways to use the energies of plant medicine and their vibrational frequencies

---

18 Herringshaw, T (ed). "Forgiveness," by Ella Giles (1890). *Local and National Poets of America: With Interesting Biographical Sketches*, US. P. 118.

Mother Earth has provided us with countless ways to use the energies of plant medicine and their vibrational frequencies in our physical, mental, emotional, and spiritual healing journeys.

in our physical, mental, emotional, and spiritual healing journeys.

Essential oils are readily available today through many distributors. Although, at the time of this writing, there is no third-party oversight for the process of growing, distilling, and distributing quality essential oils, you are asked to follow through with due diligence to find high-quality (high vibrational) essential oils that are pure and brimming with life force energy, for your highest and best good. You can measure the quality of the oil's Living Inherent Force Energy (LIFE) with a pendulum.[19]

There are many ways to include essential oils in daily life. However, for your journey through forgiveness, I will describe the process of using these oils for psycho-aromatherapeutic purposes only. These scents and frequencies can assist you on many levels, and I give their most helpful qualities pertaining to the focus at hand. The following essential oils are considered to be good choices to vibrationally support your journey through the doorways of forgiveness:

Rose

This is the highest vibrational frequency on the planet, as presently known, and can lift your spiritual vibration to the higher octaves, giving you a higher perspective. This is an opening of the crown chakra, which brings in the Soul Star energy for your soul's growth.

Frankincense

This master healing essential oil has countless therapeutic purposes. In the case of forgiveness, Frankincense is an opening to willingness. Willingness is the first step in freeing yourself from the bonds of unforgiveness. We talk about setting yourself free by forgiving others. Frankincense is the embodiment of this freedom, called willingness.

---

19 To see a live demonstration of measuring the live inherent force energy (LIFE) of essential oils, scan the QR code.

Tangerine

All the citrus essential oils open the heart and crown chakras and aligns with Angelic guidance for the process of forgiveness. Citrus, particularly tangerine, holds all of the energies described above, along with one additional gift. Tangerine (clementine) assists with the process of forgiveness—whether going through the somewhat painful process of extending forgiveness to someone who has hurt you or the need to ask for someone else to forgive you, in apology. Allow the energy of the tangerine to flow through you, to surround your energetic field, and bring higher vibrations forward in whatever way is highest and best. Tangerine holds the frequency of grace and mercy.

Lavender and Roman Chamomile

Lavender can be very helpful, along with Roman Chamomile, particularly when rigidity is involved in feelings of non-forgiveness. Lavender softens the inner gripping around the organs of the abdomen, softening the flow of the chi through the emotional center of the solar plexus. The failure to forgive is quite often a matter of emotional resistance. Both lavender and Roman chamomile can help bring peace to an overworked nervous system, assisting with trauma and mental/emotional anguish. Using these essential oils, together, is very effective.

Activation:

Forgiveness and Mother Earth

You will need a stone/rock for this Activation. This may be one of the crystals/minerals/gems we mentioned above or simply a rock you find outside on the ground. To work with a piece found in nature, ask permission from the rock before bringing it in. I generally let the area know what work I am doing, and I ask, "Who would like to do this work with me?" I then let the Nature Devas know what will happen to the piece after I am done—will it become artwork, will it sit in a comfortable place in my home, will it be returned to this spot, will it travel with me? Then, notice what "speaks" to you. One lovely piece will make itself known to you. That will be your working stone. This same process can be used from your personal collection when choosing "which" rock will be used. It is far better to work with Nature Spirits than with Google. Trust your ability to communicate with the energy field around you; this skill will grow exponentially.

What does non-forgiveness look like? How does it feel?

To get to the heart of your pain, take a moment to connect with the energy/issues that you wish to forgive or for which you seek forgiveness.

1. Sit or lie down comfortably. Take a few breaths. Close your eyes and breathe into the Earth Star chakra below and between your feet. Take a few breaths to ensure the Earth Star chakra is centered beneath and between your feet, as described above. After you are certain to be centered on this southern axis, go on to the next part.

2. Focus on the one you seek to forgive or the one from whom you seek forgiveness. Choose only one for the purpose of this exercise. See the person in your inner vision.

3. Where would that be if the energy of non-forgiveness were located somewhere within your physical body? Where is the discomfort or pain? Where are you feeling the energetic block?

4. Give it a shape. What does non-forgiveness look like? How

does it feel? Does it move? How does it move? What color is it? What is its texture? Does it make a sound? What does it sound like? Can it speak? What is it saying to you? You may want to write these answers in your journal, or you may just remember them more abstractly. Either is appropriate.

5. Place your rock on or near the shape within the body; holding your hand over it will also suffice. Feel the energy of the crystal connect and move with the energy of the shape within, they are friends, and the vibration of the shape harmonizes with the crystal.

6. Relax. Breathe with the crystal and allow the shape to move, change, shift, sound, talk, and transform. Mother Earth is healing. Your willingness is all.

7. After sitting for as long as it takes to feel a shift in energy, journal what you noticed. How has the shape changed? How large is it? What color is it now? What is the texture of the shape? Does it make a sound? What does the shape say to you now?

Messages from the Angels of Forgiveness

Chapter 12
Sacred Water

The elementals of the water kingdom are the undines—sea creatures and mer-beings. The depths of the sacred waters, represented by the water on our physical planet, hold much wisdom and healing energy and are aligned with the cardinal direction of the West. In the Platonic solids, water is represented by the icosahedron.

Being bodies of water ourselves, living on a water planet, we are deeply connected to the energy of water. Our planet and ourselves are made up of 70 percent-plus water, being affected by the

Figure 28: The element of water as represented in the Platonic solid icosahedron. (Magic Pictures/Shutterstock)

moon's phases. In our chakra system, water is the element most associated with the **sacral chakra**, the center of our creativity, procreation, and passion. There is the potential for torrential storms here, as with each of the chakras. More will be discussed about the sacral chakra in Part IV.

When working with water energy to heal the energies of non-forgiveness, we often work on a much deeper cellular level. It is a physical sea change we are seeking, so the work offered here is a deeper, more subtle energy healing.

Gem Baths

Gem baths are a profound way to internalize the beautiful energies of the mineral kingdom. Being bodies of water, no wonder soaking in water provides such terrific restorative powers to the four lower bodies—physical, emotional, mental, and etheric. Bringing your crystals, minerals, and gems into your bath transfers the energy of the mineral specimen to the entire bath and entrains the physical body to the qualities held within the mineral sample.

Note: *Some minerals cannot be used in this manner because of their composition. For example, minerals with lead content should be avoided for work with water. Be sure to research beforehand whatever you are choosing to work with.*

The following is a short list of crystals and minerals I like to use in my gem baths, but in general, all quartz will be suitable:
- Rose quartz
- Smokey quartz
- Amethyst
- Rutilated quartz
- Herkimer diamond
- Calcite

If you feel that your thoughts of non-forgiveness have magnetized unloving energies to you, you will want to get yourself clear of these energies as quickly as possible. Selenite can be a lovely way to help cleanse your energy field. Using selenite, made almost entirely of salt and calcium, in the bath will, over time, dissolve. It will first degrade, then slowly dissolve. However, you have created an ancient salt bath from crystalline salt formations created millions of years ago. This mineral is plentiful and common. Placing small pieces in your sacred bath ceremony is a terrific way to clear your physical energy of any energies you brought into your field through the Law of Vibration—"Like vibrates like." You can use the same piece for multiple baths. Bath salts (Dead Sea) or

Epsom salts (magnesium sulfate) can be very helpful and may be combined with a piece of selenite in your sacred bath.

When soaking in a gem bath, acknowledge your thoughts of unforgiveness, and invite/allow them to seep into the water to clear your physical form. When it is time to drain the water, stay in the tub and allow the water to drain away from around you—taking with it all the energy you wish to release. When you finally come out of the tub, the energy is completely gone, and you will be revitalized and refreshed in the coolness of the air.

> When soaking in a gem bath, acknowledge your thoughts of unforgiveness, and invite/allow them to seep into the water to clear your physical form.

Gem Elixirs

Water holds energy and frequency. Water is also an ideal medium for holding energy medicines. You can transfer vibrational energy from rocks and crystals into the water you drink. In fact, most charcoal filtration systems use bits of shungite and other minerals to assist in the cleansing of our drinking water. You can "program" your water with your own crystals and minerals, as well.

Place your drinking water in a sealed jar with a piece of washed and cleared quartz crystal (or other desired specimens). This container can be placed in the un-diffused morning sunlight for 30 minutes to 3 hours. Similar to a "sun tea," you are now creating an energized water that can assist in your own healing on many levels. For the specific work of forgiveness, consider using rose quartz and amethyst in your gem elixirs.

Note: *Similar to the criteria of the gem bath process, be sure that what you are using is appropriate for this work—avoiding all harmful minerals. Quartz is generally considered safe in this work, but you must be careful with many others. When in doubt, use a sealed jar inside the water container to avoid contamination. You can place fuchsite or diopside in a sealed glass jar inside the larger glass/jar of water, so the water you will drink is not directly touched by the minerals. Companies now sell sealed containers to be placed inside water bottles or carafes for convenience. However, it is often difficult to get the exact "formula" you seek—particularly for our work with forgiveness. You can create this yourself.*

Flower Essences

Flower essences are also based on the healing power of energized waters and use the energy inherent in flowers, which are here for our health and healing processes. Thanks to the insightful work of Dr. Edward Bach, we have had the benefit of using Bach Flower Essences for one hundred years now. Following in his footsteps, other companies are also creating commercially available flower essences to assist with all sorts of ailments of the four lower bodies—physical, etheric, mental, and emotional. Dr. Bach came out of the area of Western Medicine in the UK. However, native cultures worldwide and folkloric remedies have also used this process since the beginning of human history, similar to medicines of essential oils.

Flower essences are different from essential oils, and many of my clients are confused about the differences due to the use of the word "essence." Flower *essences* use the word to describe the quality of energy, the *essence* of its nature. Essential oils use the same root to describe the scent, the *essence* emitted from the plant material, and the smell. Below is a comparison of the two:

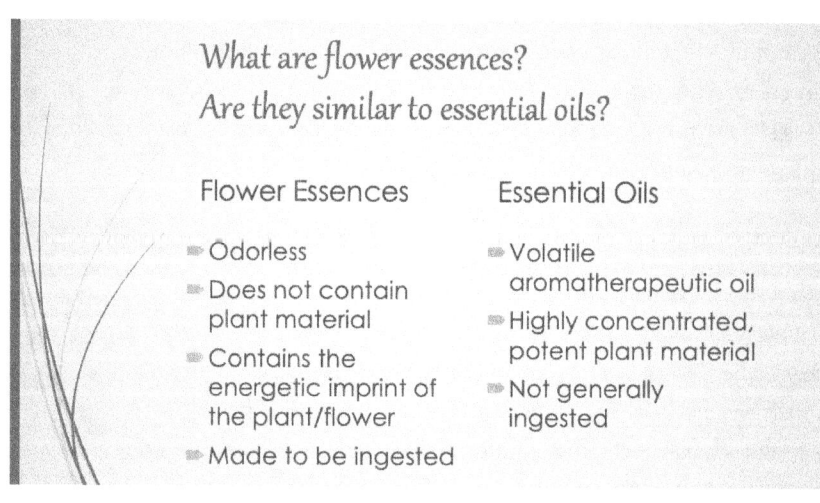

What are flower essences?
Are they similar to essential oils?

Flower Essences	Essential Oils
➡ Odorless	➡ Volatile aromatherapeutic oil
➡ Does not contain plant material	➡ Highly concentrated, potent plant material
➡ Contains the energetic imprint of the plant/flower	➡ Not generally ingested
➡ Made to be ingested	

Like gem elixirs, flower essences are energized waters meant to be ingested (although they can also be used topically or inhaled as vapor). They energetically transform places of holding and restricted flow.

Dr. Bach created a complete system of thirty-eight flower essences. The Flower Essence Society, located in California, built upon his work, adding many more. Hawaiian Rainforest Naturals, Australian Bush Flower Essences, and many other quality groups are commercially producing flower essences focusing on their local flower energies. It is a bountiful time for flower essences and energy medicine.

Coming from the tradition of Bach Flower Essences, which are readily available in stores around the globe, below is a list of flower essences that may assist with obstacles and be helpful on your forgiveness journey.

- **Star of Bethlehem**—helps heal trauma from all times and lifetimes
- **Vervain**—difficulty forgiving injustice; righteousness
- **Walnut**—overinfluenced by thoughtforms or others' energies
- **Willow**—resentments and self-pity; why me?
- **Gentian**—disappointment
- **Gorse**—given up
- **Wild rose**—resignation; dissociation from issue or self; acceptance, not forgiveness
- **Pine**—forgives others but finds it difficult to forgive self; guilt
- **Centaury**—readily forgives others, acceptance; feels deserving of poor treatment
- **Holly**—anger; rage; overwhelmed by strong emotions

When using flower essences, feel free to add them to your water, gem elixirs, your bath, or anything you are drinking. The general direction for usage is four drops, four times a day—the morning and evening being particularly supportive. Since there is no plant material in this, the energized water does not conflict with any other medications or substances you are taking. There are no contraindications in flower essences, and the system is quite easy to use without a professional practitioner. Flower essences are a highly complementary form of treatment and a beautiful gift from Mother Earth's sacred flowers.

JOURNAL
Messages from the Angels of Forgiveness

Chapter 13

The 4GiveNess Project

Week 3

Forgiving Every Body, Every Thing

This is the third meditation of The 4GiveNess Project. Do not feel rushed to move on to this week's work. Allow yourself to make your "weeks" as long as needed. This will take you further on the path of setting yourself free and releasing others, assisting you in burning karma and resolving disruptive energies on the path to ascension.

Scan the QR code to listen to the prerecorded audio of this guided meditation at any time.

Meditation

1. Allow yourself to be comfortable, sitting or lying down. Close your eyes and place your hands gently in your lap or in a meditation mudra, perhaps by joining the tip of the index finger to the tip of the thumb as a gesture of heart opening. Allow yourself to relax deeply and know that you are perfectly safe, in your space, with the Angels of Forgiveness encircling you for your wellbeing, guidance, and protection.

2. Take a deep breath, drop your awareness into the physical body, being fully present, here and now. Connect with your heart and the "I am" presence in the center of your being.

3. In the core of your physical heart is a flame—it is three flames in one, always burning. It is time to connect with that flame of Divine Presence and feel its energy, as it helps you release whatever you hold in your heart that is not love or anti-love. You may see that flame in your mind's eye in different colors. There are usually pink, blue, and gold among them. Combining, they create a Violet Flame, as well. Whatever color frequencies you are experiencing now, it is to help clear you and to balance your energy field. Allow these beautiful, flaming, life-filled colors to move through you. To help balance, nourish, shift, and energize you.

4. With every breath you take, you are fueling that flame. Connect that flame with your breath.

5. As your breath and the flame clear and balance your chakras, bring your attention to your Soul Star chakra above your crown. Feel that beautiful white light flowing through the body—that life force energy that enlivens, nourishes, and energizes you. It travels downward through each chakra, past the **root chakra**, down through the legs, down through the feet, into the Earth, connecting to your Earth Star chakra beneath your feet. As it spins and opens beautifully, the Earth Star chakra brings forward the Earth's healing energies. Those vibrations travel upward through the body, as well. In both directions, this life-force energy balances, nourishes, and enlivens you.

6. As you bring your attention back to the heart flame center, that flame fills your being and burns through the physical body and out into the auric field, transmuting everything that is not love and shifting your energies higher.

7. In your awareness, the beautifully aligned energies of the Northern and Southern Axis of the **Merkaba** and the flaming colors that are held with the vibrational flow of the

balanced Merkaba now transport you through that spirit vehicle to the beautiful Garden of Truth.

8. Take a few moments to walk through your garden. Notice what comes forward for your acknowledgment, for your awareness—without judgment, without concern—simply notice what you see, feel, sense, and know about your beautiful Garden of Truth.

9. When you are ready, find the Temple of Truth in the center of the garden.

10. You stand in front of a large staircase to the entrance. Begin moving up the stairs. You do this with ease. As you climb the steps, you realize your energies are lifted by ascending the stairs. As you look at the pillars of the sacred temple, your heart, spirit, and energy also rise. Your countenance is lifted. Your vibration is rising with every step.

11. As you go through the doors, you are warmly welcomed. You may see different people who are there. You are not alone on this journey. There are students and masters alike at the Temple of Truth. You may see them, hear them, or simply sense/know they are there.

12. On this visit to the Temple of Truth, you will find the Flame Room if you haven't already. Before you is the beautiful Flame of Truth. Find a place to sit down, relax, and feel comfortable in your own space at the Flame of Truth. The work you will do in this Flame Room is essential, as it will set you free. It will set others free as well.

13. It is time—you know it is time—to address the things you have been holding in your heart, the ways you have been hurt or harmed by the actions or decisions of others. It is time to forgive—send forgiveness to those who have harmed you. You cannot continue on this path if you hold something against another. When you are holding offense against someone else, you are the one who is bringing harm. It is time to stop the activity of attack thoughts. The Angels of Forgiveness are here to assist you. You may not

Notice what comes forward for your acknowledgment, for your awareness— without judgment, without concern.

know what it means to forgive, but they will help you—in your heart space and in your higher mind, through the energy of the Flame of Truth.

14. On the Earthly plane, in the low-density lifestream we presently experience, we have become confused by all the actions and reactions that bring about negative vibrations. And in our reactions to seeing, feeling, and experiencing the harm, the hurt, we then hold harm and hurt and think it is justified. This, in itself, keeps our karma attached to us in a way that is nearly impossible to set free and work through. We are at a beautiful point of grace, Divine Light, and Love flooding the Earth. We are given an opportunity to see what we are holding, to acknowledge our part in keeping the negative vibration alive between you and another. It is time to cut those cords and loosen our grip. Soften. Feel in your physical body now—the relaxation that comes when you loosen the grip and stop holding on to the very thing that is harming you. It is time to forgive— every body, every thing.

15. Ask for assistance from the Angels of Forgiveness. They will lead the way back to the perfection of the Divine Plan for your life, and They are here to assist you in this work. Archangel Michael is with you, as well, to help cut the cords which you are ready to bless and release. Archaea Faith is with you to assist with the vibration of your inner dialogue—the ways you create a verbal narrative that allows you to justify your inner need to hold on to the hurt. She tells you that it takes Faith to know that there is freedom on the other side of releasing this pain. Perhaps you have never felt this freedom before; have faith that it is real.

16. Stay in the presence of the Flame of Truth for several minutes as you allow images, words, and vibrations to come up and release, knowing that you are in a Divine Space of loving, healing forgiveness.

17. Feel your own energy being healed. When you set people free and release the pattern of anti-love you have held, you experience healing.

18. Feel the Flame of Truth flowing through you. Call it into your lower bodies—the physical, emotional, mental, and etheric/spiritual bodies. Allow the Flame of Truth to do its work.

19. As the Flame of Truth sets your vibration in a new alignment, in a recalibrated state, you resonate higher.

20. Raising your own vibration is not the reason we forgive. We do not forgive *because* it serves us; we forgive because it releases others. And the result is healing for all.

21. Forgive every body, every thing.

22. At this time, ask that all cords that are ready to be released, are blessed, and lovingly cut so that the energy goes back to wherever it came from—helping to make others whole once again, recalling your life force energy, as well—helping to heal the world.

23. Sit with this process for a few moments, and notice what you notice, feel what you feel.

24. With gratitude, take a deep breath and bring your awareness back to your lower bodies in the physical space. Pulling your consciousness back in, all the way down to the feet and the Earth Star chakra below you. Feel balanced, aligned, and fully energized on your Southern Axis.

25. Blink your eyes open and see the fullness of your physical surroundings. See all the shapes, colors, light, and shadows—the play of matter around you. Breathe deeply into the here and now. Notice what you notice.

Activations:
Journeys to Forgiveness

After completing the meditation, the Activations below will assist you on the journey of The 4GiveNess Project.

Sunset Journey

You are asked to connect with the energies of the natural world during this third week/cycle/season of forgiveness. We receive the sun's energies "setting" in the West daily. In truth, it is not the sun that sets at all; it is the Earth that turns away from the sun. The sunset is a glorious time of day that brings awe and wonder to the watcher. Try to connect with at least one sunset during this cycle. As you watch the movements and colors unfold before you, pull the vibrational energy of the sun into your heart and allow the sunset to energize the flame within you. Allow its energies of release to activate a sense of letting go, which liberates you from all resistance to letting go in other areas of your life. Repeat: "I let this day go; I release, let go, for the good of the world."

I let this day go; I release, let go, for the good of the world.

Waning Moon Journey

Take note of where we are in the moon cycle. The waning gibbous/third quarter moon, after the full moon and before the new moon, is a beautiful time to receive support from the moon's energies for the work of release and forgiveness. The waning moon and the third quarter phase of the moon support the energies of release, letting go, and forgiveness. Simply looking at the moon outside, or even in a picture of the moon in that final phase of the lunar cycle, before the new moon, will suffice (see figure 29).

1. Breathe in the moon's energy.
2. Feel its life force swirling through your physical body as it clears your mind and emotions.
3. Consciously pull in the moon's energies and allow them to pool in the area of the solar plexus/the stomach area—the emotional center.
4. Allow the moon's energies to clear all the disruptive emotions that tug at you from within. This is part of the re-calibration needed as you release long-held pain, disappointments, and resentments.

The meditation asks us to "Forgive every body, every thing." This is the time to search deeply within for those pieces, large and small, that you carry. It is time to address even those huge pieces as you look at your conditioned judgments of the world, for the times you silently decided never to forgive *that*.

Invite the Angels of Forgiveness to assist you so that you set yourself and others free from your own judgment. Forgiveness does not mean you accept or support the original action which caused harm, but it does mean that you will no longer actively condemn the actor. Forgive every body, every thing.

Figure 29: Waning moon.
(Lukasz Pawel Szczepanski/Shutterstock

Forgive every body, every thing.

Willing to Forgive

Do you recall when you said (out loud or with the inner voice) that you would never forgive this/that? We are often loyal to such vows. Did you keep to that promise? Can you requalify the energetic vibration of that promise and shift those words and ideas? Even if you are not yet ready to forgive "that," can you at least recall the curse of non-forgiveness that you placed upon the other person (and yourself, in the process)? Can you make an inner shift to something like, "I am willing to see this differently?" Or, even, "I am willing to revisit my un-forgiveness sometime in the future. Even that will loosen the bond you made with anti-loving energies, allowing grace to enter.

Do you recall when you judged yourself so harshly that you tacitly vowed never to forgive yourself for something? This is another form of a curse you placed in your own energetic field. These promises are even easier to keep, for we are adept at self-punishing thoughts. Can you requalify the energetic vibration of that promise and shift those words and ideas?

Speak the words, "I forgive you." Let that simple but very deep statement move through you. Feel the vibration of the words and hear your voice speaking these words. Notice what you notice. Using their/your name, "I forgive you, _____," can create space for a profound vibrational shift. Marianne Williamson, offers the following statement to assist with this process, "I forgive you _____, and I release you to the Holy Spirit."[20]

Repeating this statement regularly throughout the day can help to release your part in the vibration of attack and anti-loving thoughts, which will keep you both bound.

If you are having trouble speaking the words of forgiveness and calling that vibration with the power of your own voice and the spoken word, try writing the following statement—filling three pages of "I forgive you, _____." Allow the page to flow with this idea that comes through you and out into your visual field. There is no need to stay in/on the lines for this exercise; let the words spill out onto the page, like water covering the dry ground when it is too dense to allow it in. It may take a little while, but eventually, the ground does soften, and the water, with its nutrients and life-giving energy, is received. Notice what you notice throughout this process. Be pleased with your effort. It is good.

Cutting Cords

During this week, ask that your "cords" are cut daily. These cords keep you bound to other times, places, people, and energies. Calling in Archangel Michael and Archaea Faith will be helpful (or the Angels of Forgiveness). They will bless the cord and, as it is cut, return the life force energy to wherever it originated. Much love and compassion are involved in this process. Remember that love is never "cut," but everything you hold that is not love can be

---

20 Marianne Williamson, *A Return to Love*. (HarperOne, 1996.)

released if you lovingly request it. Only the cords you are ready to release will be cut; everything is healed in Divine Timing.

To keep the cords from reattaching, remember to use the mantra previously given: "I am undisturbed in the light of forgiveness." This is a powerful statement of commitment to the Divine Concepts of Light and Freedom.

Everything is healed in Divine Timing.

Journal

Take the time to journal or express your observations about this week's meditation and Activations creatively. This work is both intense and abstract. Sharing your experiences on the page, whether in an essay or as poetic observations, a list of words, a drawing, or other artistic expressions, can be beneficial in processing and fully realizing the experience as yours.

JOURNAL
Messages from the Angels of Forgiveness

PART IV

THE EMOTIONAL BODY

Figure 30: Icosahedron (Photo: Anne Watson)

Chapter 14

Sound, Forgiveness, and the Emotional Body

It is not uncommon to be working with a new client and find that they are energetically "covered" by thick energy that resembles layers of fur coats. This energy is heavy and dense and does not easily leave. In fact, I often ask my Angelic Guides about this dense energy, and I am told that they have placed themselves in emotional protection due to previous hurts. This may not be a choice they are consciously aware of, but out of fear, they have placed an energetic bubble wrap around themselves to protect them from others.

Figure 31: The element of sound/aether as represented in the Platonic solid dodecahedron. (Magic Pictures/Shutterstock)

Reiki and other energy healing modalities can assist in allowing energy to flow once again (see Chapter 7). However, in these instances, I am often guided to use a small musical instrument, a shaker (usually a handmade woven object with beads or seeds inside), that can break up the hard shell of energetic protection that was placed around them in an unconscious act of self-protection. After I use the shaker through their energy field and walking around them, some have reported great relief and the ability to breathe more freely. Energetic flow returns to the body and the auric field. It is at this point that I can "feel" their lower bodies and can continue with the session.

When I discuss this with clients, there is often the revelation that they have been emotionally closed to the world due to pain and trauma. You may know of people in your own life, or perhaps you have felt this yourself, who have become emotionally self-protective to the degree that they cannot let others "in." Some will even think they have forgiven others for past harms, but they want no part of a relationship with another because that would make them feel vulnerable. I have heard it said, "I have forgiven him, sure. But I will never let that happen again. I am done." We know now that that is a superficial form of forgiveness because it has not requalified the vibration of pain.

The Angels of Forgiveness tell us that "Closing off is not

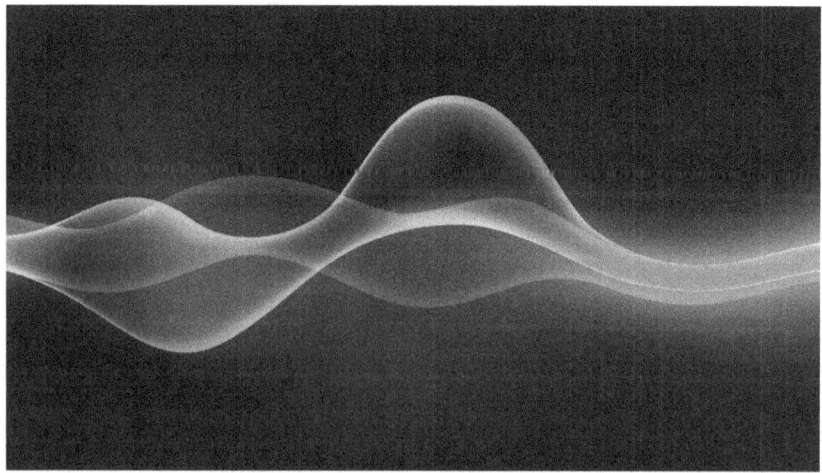

Figure 32: The rise and fall of emotional frequencies (Ioat/Shutterstock)

forgiveness." They continue that trying to use the mental body to "figure out" forgiveness in the emotional body is delusional. The Angels ask us to refrain from putting up walls to our emotional bodies, for we need all of our life force energy. Emotions will not harm us. We need to discipline our emotions to keep them from leading the way, but they have a lot to teach us if we would be willing to listen. In this chapter, we will address the feeling body, the emotional body, as a good friend rather than the enemy who has betrayed us.

Closing off is not forgiveness.

The emotional body is the vibrational you that reaches out further than any of the other bodies of your human lifeform. Your emotions resonate outward into the field, entangling with the emotional frequencies of our brothers and sisters of the Earthly plane and return strengthened by the sympathetic vibrations they resonate with on the return, as discussed in Chapter 1.

Sound waves, as shown in figure 32, are one of the ways we experience frequency. It may be helpful to realize that sound is a frequency that we can hear; however, those same frequencies also have color, and we can see them. Frequencies we *feel* are e-motions, energy in motion. Emotions are inner frequencies, yet they travel outward into the field further than our other waveforms.

Music and sound frequencies hold emotional content. We all recall times when musical works immediately brought us back to memories, thoughts, or physical sensations of previous times, simply by hearing a few familiar notes and rhythms. With just a few notes of John Williams' "dah dum, dah dum, dah dum,"[21] our emotional body resonates with the energetic image of a great white shark on the hunt or the emotion we had when we first saw this on film.

When I was hiking through the Fairy Pools on the Isle of Skye in the Scottish Highlands, I received the information I mentioned earlier in the book, which transformed my thinking

---

21 Steven Spielberg, John Williams & John Williams. JAWS. USA (1975)

and connection to the elements and elementals. I was "told" that, for the purposes of growth and healing, I needed to understand that there is a fifth element, which is not as understood earlier. I was told that the fifth element was sound. I was then told that sound was a natural force on earth, like fire, air, earth, and water, that held matter together.

I was shown that sound was such a fundamental force of nature that it is often overlooked because we think of it as having influence only through the ear. However, sound vibration holds all matter together; it is sound vibration that moves matter. Nothing happens without sound; whether we hear it with our physical ears or not, it is felt and resonates indefinitely. We often consider sound to be the result of a movement—the consequence of moving air, the result of the Earth's movements, fire burning its fuel, the waves crashing to the shore. However, I am told sound can actually *create* movement—that sound is the action of the prime mover. Our sacred texts remind us, "In the beginning was the Word, and the Word was with God, and the Word was God." [22]

Sound is the fifth element of creation; perhaps it is the first. Sound is aligned with the quality of presence and the direction of that above and below you as it flows *through* you along the vibrational axis of the chakral column. Sound becomes/is your central axis. The elemental beings of sound

Figure 33: The vibrational axis of the chakral column
(Irina Ashpina/Shutterstock)

22 John 1:1.

are the Angels—the Divine Messengers who bring sound and song through all beings. In the Platonic solids, the dodecahedron represents the universe or aether; I am guided to utilize this as the sound of the universe.

There is much written about sound healing and the powerful effects of humming and toning to release blocked energy within the physical body. The vibrations from the body resonate throughout the physical form, allowing one to move stuck energy in very effective ways. It is also the activity with the opposite outcome— the words and tones we produce which are unloving or unkind will resonate with those vibrations, as well. Quite simply, we are what we speak.

When I am in a state of non-forgiveness, or when something I had tried to forgive returns to my awareness, it is most often an emotional message. I will emotionally feel dysregulated or agitated. Identifying where the message lives within your being is a big step in the direction of taking responsibility for it and ultimately being able to shift its vibrational resonance. Emotions do not need to hijack your intentions if you understand their messages and usher them into places where they can be most constructive.

Sound is the fifth element of Creation; perhaps it is the first.

Our energetic resonance, as both transmitters and receivers, makes us transceivers—we project outwardly and receive inwardly through the furthermost body of our being, the emotional body. Cleansing the emotional body becomes an important part of our ability to forgive well.

Activation:
Toning

There is a tone being played, struck, or sung. As a musician in this life, you have a few options:

1. You can match the tone.
2. You can harmonize with the tone, playing a different tone (or many) that sound/feel complimentary or antagonistic— consonant or dissonant.
3. You remain silent.

And so it is in life. This is the action/reaction response played out daily, every day. The unforgiving vibration is found as a possibility in the last two. The first one might be a peaceful reply; however, it is not necessarily peace, for it could mean you are giving up and simply following. Without regard to intention, the only truly objectively loving response is found in the second response, harmony with consonance. This is harmonious.

Whenever we come into contact with dissonant and disruptive sounds, whether it is the cutting down of tree limbs, street cleaners, grating sink disposals, or a shrieking child, I am shown that the quickest way to peace is to "match" the tone. Whether you hum, sing, or internalize the tone with your quiet inner voice, find a complementary tone that fills out the disruptive sound by creating a bit of harmonious music. When you stop singing/humming/inwardly toning, the disruption is diminished. It no longer grates at your nervous system and no longer affects you as it did before. You have taken the time to embody the original tone and offered a compassionate partnership in harmony.

Activation:
Call and Response

The next time you are in the presence of an unpleasant, unpeaceful sound made by either human or a machine, try the Call and Response exercise described above by doing the following:

1. Hum or sing the *perceived tone* of the sound as it is. Even if it isn't a "tone," per se, find its qualitative frequency. Give it a try. Practice with these:
   - What is the tone of the following statement: "My dear [*insert your name*], I have missed you very much. I'm so glad you are here." Feel (or guess) the frequency and sing or hum it. *What do you feel?*
   - Then, what is the tone of this statement: "Hey, you! Yeah, you. Move it. Get out of the way!" Feel the frequency and

sing or hum it. *What do you feel?*

- Now . . . listen to your environment right now. What are you hearing? Choose just one thing and match its tone. Give it a hum or a vocalized tone. Match its frequency. *What do you feel?*

2. Now, staying with the tone in your surroundings, allow your voice to slide upward into a complementary tone. It doesn't matter what the specific note or tone is; let your voice rest where it "feels" good and comfortable. Find the inherent beauty between the original sound in your environment and the second tone (the one you are offering). Hear both tones at once—this is a **chord**. Hold this chord for several seconds; 10 - 15 seconds will do nicely.

3. Gently stop toning. As you release this chord, allow the vibrations to resonate through you and notice how you feel now.

4. As you listen to your environment, what has changed for you? Journal about your observations.

5. Continue this exercise as you notice the sounds of your environment coming into your emotional space.

This is the practice of emotional forgiveness with sound. You have heard the tone, really heard it, understood it, and allowed it to resonate through you. Then, you offered a harmonic resolution. According to the Angels of Forgiveness, this *is* forgiveness. This practice is transformative and will invite great shifts in those areas of emotional discord with just a bit of dedicated practice.

The Call from Within

The Call and Response activation described above can be an effective tool within your own system, as well. Consider your non-forgiveness, whether for yourself, another, or the world itself. Allow your thoughts to evoke emotions, knowing they are never far away. Notice "where" the emotions live within you. Often, this is a place where your system is vulnerable; it may even be where illness tends to reside.

You have heard the tone, really heard it, understood it, and allowed it to resonate through you. Then, you offered a harmonic resolution. According to the Angels of Forgiveness, this *is* forgiveness.

Take a moment now to scan your physical being with a hum. Move the energy of the hum through all parts of your body, to every muscle, organ, gland, bone, and joint, to every sinew of your being.

Find where the sound "catches," gets stuck, is resistant, or merely feels dull. Listen to this change in energy and allow your voice to connect with the vibration within you at this point which is making itself known to you now.

Give that place attention with your voice. It may change into another sound, no longer a hum, but a vocalization, breath, or percussive mouth sound. Without judgment or fear, give that place its voice and time. Stay with it, unhurried. Really hear it out.

At some point, this sound will reveal another impulse. Often this is met with an uplifting toning or something like a sung tone. Allow the song to develop without force or plan. Just let it be what it is to become. Hear that, as well.

Once the energy has changed, return to your scanning with the hum. Continue this until you find the next place that reveals itself to you. Then go inside that place and listen deeply.

This transformative work offers much to the giver/receiver, you. Here is a summary of the steps for Inner Call and Response Work:

1. Before you begin, notice the overall comfort and ease of your emotional body. On a scale of one to ten, how tight is your emotional energy? Quite simply, how are you *feeling*?

2. See yourself in your mind's eye and your kinesphere (the circle of energy surrounding you, as if you were a planet). Conduct a scan of the area surrounding you (within 10–20 feet or so) with your voice.[23]

3. When you find a place that is not smooth or clear, stay a while, and let your voice communicate with that area. Allow

---

23 Although we are introducing this, here, as a clearing for the emotional body, this work can also be done as a scan of the physical body, "sending" the voice through areas of the physical body. As a scan of the etheric body, one might want to send the voice through the chakra system. As a scan of the mental body, allow the voice to move through the mind, with eyes closed, and allow your thoughts to vibrate up, with the tones.

your voice to become the voice of the disruption. Notice how your voice changes. Without judgment, allow the voice to become the voice of this pattern. Respect what it has to say.

4. After a while (this may be 15 seconds or 15 minutes), the energy will shift and release from this area, and there will be an impulse to rise into something of a tone, note, or song. Let your voice rise with the energy. This is the healing you seek.

5. Take a moment to allow your full being to assimilate the energetic changes. Take note of how you feel. On a scale of one to ten, how energetically/emotionally tight are you now? Hold it gently.

6. Continue with scanning as time allows. Sometimes, doing this work in smaller chunks, perhaps focusing on one area at a time, might be a more comfortable way to work. However, I do suggest you move on to find the next area that needs to be heard if you are able.

7. Taking a couple of moments to journal your experiences can reveal patterns and underlying energetic connections that otherwise might go unnoticed.

8. On a scale of one to ten, how tight is your body's energetic flow now?

Entraining to the Music of the Universe

Classical musical theory is described by the Roman philosopher and statesman Boethius, who lived 480–524 CE. In his treatise, *De Institutione Musica,* Boethius describes three major forms of music experienced by humans: *Musica Mundana, Musica Humana, and Musica Instrumenta Constituta. Musica Mundana* is the musical sound of the universe, which we perceive as the vibrational result of celestial bodies in orbit, the structure of the elements, or the changing seasons. Pythagoras coined this type of sound as the "Music of the Spheres," later used by Shakespeare and other philosophers and writers sensitive to the whirring tones of life in motion.

The second form of music, according to Boethius, is *Musica Humana*. This is the music of the human being within the physical form, necessitating a certain harmony within the physical body and its field. Much research has gone into the movement of energy surrounding the physical body, its electromagnetic field, and the electromagnetic field of particular spheres, such as the heart and other organs.

The third form, for Boethius' study of music, is *Musica Instruemntis Constituta*. This is instrumental music played by breath, striking, vibrational tension, or even those activated by water or gravitational force. This is a human-made instrument, creating sound and enjoyed through the ear and physical form as a receiver of the sound.

The ideas of Boethius and Pythagoras find their way through literature and philosophy. Shakespeare is quite complete in his description of the ideas in *The Merchant of Venice* (c. 1600):

Lorenzo

How sweet the moonlight sleeps upon this bank.
Here will we sit and let the sounds of music
Creep in our ears; soft stillness and the night
Become the touches of sweet harmony.
Sit, Jessica. Look how the floor of heaven
Is thick inlaid with patens of bright gold.
There's not the smallest orb which thou behold'st
But in his motion, like an angel sings,
Still choiring to the young-eyed cherubins.
Such harmony is in immortal souls,
But whilst this muddy vesture of decay
Doth grossly close it in, we cannot hear it.
Enter Stephano and musicians.
Come, ho! and wake Diana with a hymn.
With sweetest touches pierce your mistress' ear,
And draw her home with music.

[Music plays.]

JESSICA

I am never merry when I hear sweet music.

LORENZO

The reason is, your spirits are attentive.

For do but note a wild and wanton herd

Or race of youthful and unhandled colts,

Fetching mad bounds, bellowing and neighing loud,

Which is the hot condition of their blood,

If they but hear perchance a trumpet sound,

Or any air of music touch their ears,

You shall perceive them make a mutual stand,

Their savage eyes turned to a modest gaze

By the sweet power of music. Therefore the poet

Did feign that Orpheus drew trees, stones,

and floods,

Since naught so stockish, hard, and full of rage,

But music for the time doth change his nature.

The man that hath no music in himself,

Nor is not moved with concord of sweet sounds,

Is fit for treasons, stratagems, and spoils;

The motions of his spirit are dull as night,

And his affections dark as Erebus.

Let no such man be trusted. Mark the music.[24]

---

24 William Shakespeare, *The Merchant of Venice*, Act V, Scene 1

The Frequency of Forgiveness

There is a particular frequency, a specific tone that can assist in helping us shift through holding patterns of non-forgiveness. This frequency is 639Hz. In general, this aligns with the solfeggio note of "Re" or a D. Within the chakral system, this tone generally aligns with the sacral chakra, the seat of passion, sexuality, and creativity. In Sanskrit, the sacral chakra is called "Svadhisthana," which is often translated to mean sweetness. Looking at the literal components of the "Swa" means one's own, and "Adhisthana" means abode or seat. Many refer to the sacral chakra as the seat of the soul. The qualities of this energy center are feminine, watery, and connected to the moon. No wonder this chakra is the doorway to the emotional body.

In sound healing treatments, I use two tuning forks, holding a frequency of 639Hz, to bring the energy through and around the physical body, sending the healing tones throughout the electromagnetic field and the outermost emotional body. Like the Call and Response exercise earlier, I seek those places in and around the four lower bodies that do not feel clear within the presence of this tone. Those are the areas where I linger, listen, and lean in, with Reiki and sound healing energies.

Many refer to the sacral chakra as the seat of the soul. The qualities of this energy center are feminine, watery, and connected to the moon.

Activation:
639Hz Frequency

The 639Hz frequency is a vibration of love, communication, and unity and can assist with relationship understanding and creating tolerance and harmony. Toning the 639Hz frequency while meditating on a particular situation or person you seek to release from non-forgiveness can be very effective and freeing for all. You might want to obtain your own tuning forks; however, I have created a 5-minute track for you here, so you can feel, meditate, and tone with 639Hz.

As you listen to the frequency, imagine (see or feel) that this tone is coming from the full moon. Sense its light and tone connecting with your emotional body to clear, purify, and refresh all that is held there for your highest and best good.

While sitting with 639Hz, journal about your feelings and what the tone vibrates for you. Below is what the tone brought up and through for me:

Stinging through the physical form
The ears, the eyes, the hands,
and then
the heart
Deeper still
Still
Stillness of the soul
Deeper to the core
Swimming through leagues of tension
Resistance
Pressure
Still
Shoulders, jaw, and belly ache to let it go
To heal within without
Still
Loosening
Joy
A pinpoint of light
Is this me?
Still
NotmeWe
A single point of one
weareweareweareweare639
weareweareweone
Vibrato variation a tone of tones of tone
Fading smallest of waves
Outward
Returning to self
Still
~639Hz

Activation:
Forgiveness Playlist

Music, like sound, can be immensely healing, as it soothes our being—body, mind, and spirit, on a mystical level. As you listen to music, remember what you learned about toning, and give yourself permission to hum or sing along. Allow yourself the freedom to feel the emotions and sing through them. Remember that e-motion is energy in motion and allow yourself the freedom to move and dance with it, as well. If emotions rise, let the tears fall, the laughter rise, and allow it to flow. Let go of any fear of emotions you may have.

E-motion is energy in motion.

Here is a short list of musical compositions that may assist you on this journey:

- Haydn, *Seven Last Words*
- Arvo Part, *Spiegel Im Spiegel*
- Arvo Part, *Solfeggio*
- Claude Debussy, *Claire De Lune*
- Laurie Anderson, *Flow*
- India Arie, *Wings of Forgiveness*
- TobyMac, *Forgiveness*
- Alicia Keys, *Pray for Forgiveness*
- Matthew West, *Forgiveness*
- Prince, *Purple Rain* (a personal fave)

Write your own shortlist of musical pieces or inspirational sounds that resonate with your personal frequency of forgiveness below. Taking a moment to ponder your playlist may assist you in the future, as well, so you can access these when you need support for the mystical musical journey:

The Sound of Laughter

The research is clear that humor, and individuals who demonstrate a more positive perspective, have an easier time forgiving others.[25] Without "making light" of some difficult and traumatic experiences that you may have been through in working with the energetic disruptions in the emotional body, humor is indeed good medicine.

The Angels of Forgiveness confirm that laughter clears the emotional body. Although there are many genres of humor, and contemporary comedy can be of the stinging sort, I want to be clear that we are talking specifically about self-enhancing and non-aggressive humor. Laughter clears the emotional body like nothing else can.

Laughter clears the emotional body like nothing else can.

The sound of laughter can be a very good start. A quick minute on your local search engine can easily connect you with the "sounds of laughter" that will help to clear the emotional body and the second and third chakras.

Have you ever noticed how you feel after spending time in the presence of someone's good humor? Their exuberance and willingness to share laughter are cleansing and healing. Good humor cleanses the energy field and the emotional bodies of all nearby.

Can't get in touch with your college friend that would have you rolling on the floor, clutching your abdominal chakras? Blessings to streaming services with oodles of comedy, even the older shows and movies that were less harsh and biting. I like the goofy movies of the seventies and eighties. Although I may be watching them without my friends, I will be laughing.

The highest and best activity, though, would be to engage in humor in your daily life, allowing yourself to laugh more and to delight in the humor that everyday living in the world provides.

25 Hampes, William. (2016). "The Relationship Between Humor Styles and Forgiveness." Published under creative commons use and housed at the National Institutes for Health (NIH), National Library of Medicine. https://www.ncbi.nlm.nih.gov/pmc/articles/PMC4991043/

We can become so very serious and frustrated as we move through our task-filled schedules. Perhaps it is time to schedule a bit of laughter to help you heal and clear your emotional body. The world will thank you.

Activation:
Laugh Laboratory

Training yourself to laugh more freely may be easier than you think. That's because it is not a thought-body process; it is the work of the emotional body. Try this:

1. Find a place where you will be undisturbed for a few minutes, where you will not be heard, as well. Sometimes your car will be the perfect laugh laboratory.
2. Notice how you feel and the tension within and around you.
3. Bring forward a memory or image you find humorous, ridiculous, or absurd. This could be something you experienced or saw second-hand happening to someone else. Perhaps you will recall the last time you had a good laugh. For some, it will take a bit of time to recall last having a good laugh. If this is your experience, you may want to start keeping a running list of the funny or absurd events you witness in life. This will help you to shift your outlook as you seek the uplifting in your life and look for the fun.
4. Hold the energy of the humorous situation and take a deep belly breath. Feel the emotion come alive once again within your physical body.
5. On the exhale, begin to laugh. At first, it will feel forced, but that will let go when your conscious judging mind does. Stay with the laugh for a few seconds, perhaps longer. Can you sustain this laughing exercise for twenty seconds or more?
6. Allow it to come to a natural rest.
7. Sometimes other emotions will piggyback with the waves of laughter. Let all the emotions come up, for they are letting you know they are there.

8. At the end of the laugh laboratory session, note how you feel and the level of tension within and around you.

10. More importantly, though, notice how you feel for the next few hours.

Note: The Laugh Laboratory activation can be done with others in a group setting where members feel safe and comfortable with each other. Lying down, with each person, placing their head on the abdomen of another, when one person begins to laugh, it becomes a contagion of laughter, as the movement travels from one to the next and back again, creating its own e-motional transfer.

JOURNAL
Messages from the Angels of Forgiveness

Chapter 15

The 4GiveNess Project

Week 4

The Zeal of Truth

In *A Course in Miracles*, it says, "The Real world is attained simply by the complete forgiveness of the old, the world you see without forgiveness."[26] And as a bridge between Divine Father and Mother Earth, you have the opportunity to release your hold on the misqualified energies of the old world, the human-made systems found on Earth—all the ways humankind has been misled by its own misunderstandings of itself. We have learned about who we are from our human mothers and fathers, our families and friends, our teachers, our belief systems, institutions, governments, societies, cultures, etc. It is now time to reach higher, through the Flame of Truth, to learn of the original perfection of the Divine Concept, which still flows through each and every one of us.

---

26 *A Course in Miracles*, 17: II, 5

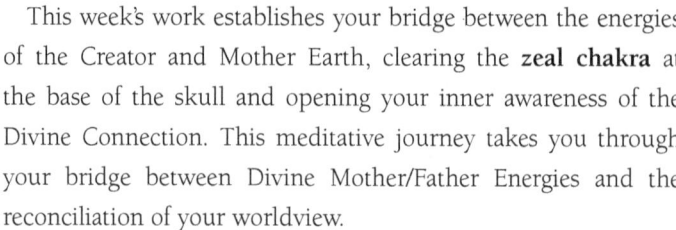

Forgiveness: Journey to a clear place

As a bridge between Divine Father and Mother Earth, you have the opportunity to release your hold on the misqualified energies of the old world, the human-made systems found on Earth.

This week's work establishes your bridge between the energies of the Creator and Mother Earth, clearing the **zeal chakra** at the base of the skull and opening your inner awareness of the Divine Connection. This meditative journey takes you through your bridge between Divine Mother/Father Energies and the reconciliation of your worldview.

Scan the QR code to listen to the prerecorded audio of this guided meditation at any time.

Meditation

1. Create a sacred space where you will not be disturbed. Light a candle and find a comfortable place to sit or lie down. Settle into the physical body and allow yourself to fully arrive in the here and now. Tell your body, "It is time to relax."

2. With each breath, allow yourself to draw your awareness into the center of the body, more fully, more deeply. Spend a few moments with the energies of the heart.

3. Take a moment to connect with the energy center of the Earth Star chakra, which connects with the energies of Mother Earth. As you breathe with Mother Earth, connect with the image of the veins of gold flowing through the Earth.

4. Allow the balancing energies of golden light to ascend upward, flowing through each of the chakras, through the midline of the body: the root chakra, the sacral chakra, the solar plexus, the heart, the **throat chakra**, the zeal chakra, the **brow/third eye chakra**, and the crown chakra, all the way up to the Soul Star chakra—connecting you to energies of the golden light of the Great Sun.

5. You are here, now, between Mother Earth and Divine Father. You are the bridge between the two Divine Concepts. Just as you came into this physical body in the world of form with a joining of mother and father energies, you bridge and bring those energies forward with you continually, with

every breath, with every thought, with every action, you are ever fully connected and extending those energies outward.

6. Around you, now, you see/feel/sense/know the Merkaba gently spinning around you, balanced and steady—clearing the chakras and holding your space.

7. Know that in your room, the beautiful Angels of The 4GiveNess Project—Archangels and Ascended Masters surround you. Know that the Divine Beings of your personal belief system are also present as your Creator, Mother-Father God, supports and energizes your journey to freedom.

8. As your Merkaba is spinning and balancing you—it is bringing you to your sacred garden. See, feel, sense, and know that you are being brought there now. As the scene becomes more real to you, you see all the colors of the garden, you hear the sounds, you feel the temperatures and textures on your skin, and the flow of energy through this garden, through you. Scan the garden and the surroundings. Notice what you notice.

9. Being familiar with the garden by now, you find your way to the sacred Temple of Truth in the center of the garden. You climb the stairs and enter the temple. Notice what comes into your awareness.

10. You are led and brought to the beautiful Flame Room. This is the room that holds the sacred Flame of Truth. However it appears to you, it is a sacred, Divine Fire. It is not destructive, but it transmutes energy and raises its vibration. Find a place to sit down and merge with this beautiful Flame of Truth.

11. As this flame lives and breathes before you, you may begin to see, hear, feel, sense, or know of those specific times your anger, disappointment, or frustration was directed at systems, institutions, or laws that you did not agree with. What about the outer physical world? Have you found it difficult to forgive? Notice how your reaction, your own response, brings a lower vibration into the field to an

already difficult situation.

12. As you think of these somewhat unforgivable laws, systems, institutions, and dogmas, see how your own reaction, your own response, brings lower vibrations into the field to an already difficult situation. This reaction, this response, is part of the complexity. In this situation, it is time to ask for forgiveness for how you have re-acted and brought lower vibrations into the world, participating in non-love and the lack of light. Simply bring those times, those responses forward, in asking for forgiveness in the vibrational field. "My reaction, my response did not bring light. Please forgive me. For all those times when my own response, my own reaction did not bring light, I ask forgiveness."

13. Notice how you feel. Notice how the vibrations change within you and around you. Sit in those shifting energy for a few moments.

14. You also have an opportunity to forgive the system, the institution, and the world for not being the way you wanted it to be. "I forgive the world. I forgive the system. I forgive the institution for not being the way I wanted it to be." Notice the inner release, the softening that rises. This is necessary, for if you continue to hold negative thoughts about the world and its laws, you will not be able to participate effectively in the change and transformation that needs to take place. We must forgive the world for not being as we wanted it to be. To change and bring harmony, you must hold a different tone.

15. At this moment, in front of the beautiful Flame of Truth, release your hold on your own judgment. Your judgment does not bring healing. Release your hold on your righteousness. Release your hold by extending forgiveness by receiving forgiveness—for giving and receiving are the same action.

16. Forgive the world for being the way it is. Forgive the world for being the way it is, so you may assist in the coming

transformation. "I am willing to see the truth. I am willing to see things differently. I am willing to forgive the world for being the way it is."

17. If you have been holding Mother-Father God, Divine Creator, Source responsible for the world being the way it is, it is time to release that judgment, that disappointment, that righteousness. Set yourself free from the system of judgment; it keeps you trapped in the very energy that you wish to escape. "I forgive the world for being the way it is."

18. Release your hold. Release your grip. Release your judgment. Release yourself by extending forgiveness.

19. Allow the burning Flame of Truth to enter into the zeal chakra at the base of the skull, where hardwiring and the acceptance of that which is not true have been residing within your energetic system. Allow the Flame of Truth to release all hardwiring at this time, opening that chakra/portal to its original purpose of Higher Connection—the connection to Divine Truth. The Flame of Truth will now transmute the lower vibrations of human misdirection and dysfunctional patterns in the zeal chakra. Notice what you notice.

20. The Divine Presence within the Three-Fold Flame of the heart begins to expand and rise up to meet the energies of the Flame of Truth at the zeal chakra. And you feel a rising within your own vibrational field. The flames connect and become one—love, wisdom, strength, and truth.

21. Instead of connecting with the misqualified and misdirected perceptions of this life, in the world of matter, you are becoming attuned to truth. Allow that to move through you and out into the vibrational field, transmuting all misqualified energies, releasing all confusion, and bringing peace.

I forgive the world for being the way it is.

22. You may feel, notice, and experience the beautiful blessings of the Angels of Forgiveness as they step forward and place their energetic hands over your head into your vibrational

field, bringing a blessing of light. This blessing requalifies lower frequencies, allowing the cords to your karmic past to be severed and removing all hardwiring that you are ready to release, helping you to reach a greater balance than you had before. This is a sacred blessing of forgiveness and mercy, and it is yours to draw into your being and to share on your path with more clarity, balance, and grace.

Your willingness to forgive is the blessing you receive now.

23. You have, in this sacred space, the ability to feel/receive this gift of grace and to share it with all of Earth, to send it "out" to all who would accept it. This is a blessing for the human condition. Send the **Law of Forgiveness** out through your heart center, through the zeal chakra of higher communication, and out through the Merkaba of the electromagnetic field surrounding you, for this connects you most directly to the Spirit of One.

24. Knowing that you can come back to this beautiful Flame of Truth to meet with the Angels of Forgiveness at any time to gain clarity, insight, and higher vibrational blessings, we will allow the Merkaba to bring us back to the awareness of the physical body in your physical space. Connect with the Earth Star chakra beneath your feet, pulling all of the higher frequencies back into the physical body, anchoring it to the Earth directly where you are. For you are that bridge, that channel, that conduit between Heaven and Earth, and you call that energy in to bless the Earth and all of humanity—holding space between Mother Earth and Divine Father, in balance, not to be moved by the outward circumstances or appearances. For you are aware of the higher truth and are a demonstration of the grace of forgiveness.

You are the bridge between two Divine concepts

25. Thank you to all Divine Beings, Mother Earth, and Divine Father for the blessings of truth and forgiveness.

Meditation Response:

After experiencing the meditative journey, look at the list you created in Chapter 1 (see page 51), where you listed the people/situations you have difficulty forgiving. Has there been any change in your emotional body? Can you find some new inner space between your emotional response to the items on the list and the Higher Truth of the human condition? Does this inner space feel like compassion?

In the space provided, respond to your original list in light of the meditation for this week. Also, at this point in your journey, how do you see/experience/receive the creative expression (the drawing/painting/song, etc.) you created about the shadow places of non-forgiveness?

If your list still burns hot with anger, rage, indignation, or any level of disappointment, consider taking the meditative journey again. Keep working with this larger frame of forgiveness until a softening of the heart helps you release the knots that keep you bound to your list. Recognize that forgiveness is not acceptance or support for harm but a compassionate release of blame so that you can participate in what needs to be done for healing to begin. For that to happen, we all participate in raising the energy field.

What will change when you can truly forgive the world for being what and how it is?

What will change when you can truly forgive the world for being what and how it is?

Prayer: Forgiveness for the World

Dear Mother-Father God,
We thank you for giving a direct connection to Your light
within each and every one of us.
In gratitude, we seek to bring our minds, hearts, and souls
into alignment with your Divine Truth.
Please teach us how to hear your clear voice of love and guidance.
Please show us how to feel the Divine Presence within each of us.
Please show us how to experience this world differently,
beyond appearances, as it truly is, in your Light.
In gratitude, we sing,
Aum-Amen

JOURNAL
Messages from the Angels of Forgiveness

Chapter 16

The 4GiveNess Project

Week 5

In the Clear Place

The paradox of the journey to a clear place is that it is not a way of paths or turns, but it is a journey within. No matter how often we shift the icosahedron, we are still on the outside looking in. The journey to the clear place is to, one day, find yourself inside, looking outward. Centered. Whole. Knowing the truth of your being from the inside out. The clear place is the place of being, and the journey is a journey of becoming.

> The clear place is the place of being, and the journey is a journey of becoming.

The Angels of Forgiveness are quite pleased with every effort you make to become clear, and their support on this journey is unwavering. These beautiful Divine Messengers would like to gift you one final transmission of great light for the journey ahead. In this final meditation of "The 4GiveNess Project," you will receive a gift from the Angels of Forgiveness, so you will be able to develop a deep connection with the Angels of Forgiveness for ongoing guidance through the daily flow of release and Divine love.

Scan the QR code to listen to the prerecorded audio of this guided meditation at any time.

Meditation

1. Create a quiet space for yourself where you will not be disturbed. Light a candle, and make yourself comfortable, sitting on the floor or in a chair with your legs folded or your feet flat on the ground.

2. Take a deep breath, and gently bring awareness to your heart center. Breathe deeply into the heart and allow yourself to feel and experience everything you hold within it—all the love you have ever known in this lifetime and every other lifetime.

3. Tell your body that it is time to relax now, knowing that this is your time set aside to work on self-love.

4. In your mind's eye, place yourself in your sacred garden that is now so familiar. You have been here many times.

5. What comes to your awareness? Whatever catches your attention, lean in and take a closer look. Notice the new growth in the garden. How do you feel as you experience this garden now? Notice what you notice.

6. As the scene unfolds, you find a body of water—a pond, a stream, or even a waterfall. Go to the water's edge and find a beautiful place to sit and relax. Feel yourself relax more fully listening to the water, feeling the moisture in the air. As you sit in the garden by the water, ponder the flow of forgiveness.

7. The you sitting by the water breathes deeply into their heart center. And in their consciousness, they walk through the garden, and they place themself in a beautiful area by the sacred Temple of Truth in the middle of the garden. And that version of yourself finds a beautiful place to sit outside the temple. Feeling the energy of the Temple of Truth, they may be touching the marble and wood, seeing the rocks, gemstones, artwork, and decoration outside the temple.

Feeling this energy moving through them, uplifting.

8. In their meditation, as they close their eyes and breathe deeply, they connect to their heart center. Feeling love. In their consciousness, they see an inner version of themselves walking up the steps of the Temple of Truth and entering the sacred space. They make their way to the Flame Room, where they sit beside the Flame of Truth. That beautiful green-gold-white flame.

9. That inner version of yourself settles into a deeper meditation beside the Flame of Truth. With their eyes closed and connecting with their heart, they ponder, forgiving every body every thing.

10. They allow the Flame of Truth to burn through their energy body. They allow their awareness to rise and feel their consciousness expanding to a higher vibrational plane. They rise into the etheric/energetic plane, lifted by the atoms and the electrons of the air, into a finer energy, a more refined vibration, and they connect with a version of themselves we will call the Higher Self. This version of you has already ascended into Divine Light Consciousness. This is you. Already ascended. Beyond time and space. This is you. Connecting. Here and now.

11. This version of you is surrounded by Angelic Beings emanating musical vibrations, songs of higher love, and Divine Light. This light and sacred sound will lead you the rest of the way; follow their guidance.

12. This version of yourself is connected to Divine Consciousness, to the Divine Plan, and has beautiful messages of love, strength, and wisdom to share with you. This is a place of non-judgment. This higher vibration is without judgment. You have reached a place beyond judgment. It is a place where forgiveness is not necessary—beyond forgiveness, the clear place. In this refined state, there is nothing to forgive. Forgiveness is needed for those who judge. Forgiveness is extended by

those who carry judgment within their heart. When you hold nothing but love, there is no judgment, and there is no need for Forgiveness. There is no separation. It is a place of Divine Wholeness. Oneness. Beyond perspective. Beyond forgiveness.

13. .The Angels of Forgiveness will now place a beautiful crystalline structure, an icosahedron, into the heart center, as a symbol of your Divine Consciousness within.

14. What does that feel like in your heart now? What do you notice? Notice those parts of you that are resistant. Bring love. That, too, can be healed. Bring love to those parts of you that resist moving beyond the need to forgive.

15. Allow your Higher Self to bring forward anything you need to know about the grace of moving beyond forgiveness, beyond judgment, and beyond the need for forgiveness. Remain open and receptive. Remain here as long as you feel inwardly guided.

16. Reaching this version of yourself, the Higher Self, this blessing, is something you can do regularly. In all reality, this is just a thought away.

17. In this moment, we will say thank you to your Higher Self for the guidance, the wisdom, the experience, the glimpse of a moment without judgment—a moment beyond forgiveness. This is the path; this is possible.

18. With gratitude, the version of you sitting at the sacred Flame of Truth takes a deep breath and pulls the energy of the Higher Self back into yourself. That version of you opens their eyes.

19. That version of you that sits outside the Temple of Truth takes a deep breath and pulls the version of themselves from the Flame Room back into themselves, fully aware and awake, opening their eyes.

20. The version of you that sits in the garden by the water takes a deep breath and pulls the version of self that was sitting outside the temple back into themself, fully. Bringing all

that energy from the Higher Self, from the Flame Room Self, from the outer Temple Self, back into the fullness of their experience in the garden by the body of water. You feel yourself expanding with each awakening.

21. And as that version of you that sits at the water opens their eyes, you take a deep breath and pull your consciousness back in completely, drawing in that version of you sitting in the garden by the water. And pull all of the life force energy of all parts of yourself back into you, into the here and now. And feel your heart expanding to hold the higher vibrations of the Higher Self.

22. Holding, in this physical form, the memory of a space within you that is beyond judgment, beyond forgiveness—into Divine Wholeness. Connection. One.

23. As you connect with the Earth Star chakra beneath your feet, there is one more awakening within. You gently blink your eyes open and connect with the play of matter around you in your physical room. Seeing all the shapes and colors, the light and shadows around you. Your perception and perspective.

24. Notice what you notice. How do you feel? What are you aware of?

25. May you experience much peace and love.

You have reached a place beyond judgment. It is a place where forgiveness is not necessary—beyond forgiveness, the clear place.

Meditation Response

This journey is ultimately one of higher connection—reaching the Higher Ascended Self, which is within you. What do you want to recall or continue to process about this experience? Write a description of the experience, a poem, a list of words, or draw a picture that helps you capture the essence of your meditation experience.

What does it mean to you to be "beyond forgiveness?" Do you see this as possible? What will you experience (what will change in your life) when you release judgment and get to the place where there is nothing to forgive?

Activation:
Be-Coming Forgiveness
We have come to this point in the journey where it is not necessary to engage in any action of the outer physical world to determine the clarity of your inner light. You have, indeed, overcome the world with the inner awakening of the Higher Self. You now know, on all levels of your being, that the grace of the God-Presence within is the font of forgiveness. What else is there to *do*? Nothing. My friends, we *are* the clear place of forgiveness.

Prayer for Awakening in Forgiveness

Dear Mother-Father God,
Thank you for the light of Your forgiveness
that flows through the four lower bodies of each of us.
We patiently hold space for the awakening of all beings
as we transform this world together in the light of forgiveness.
Brother-to-brother, friend-to-friend, we rise as One
before the dawn to witness the new day
and the transformation be-coming.
In gratitude, we sing,
Aum Amen

JOURNAL
Messages from the Angels of Forgiveness

Chapter 17

Afterward: Forgiveness Activism

Forgiveness in My Story

My parents left this planet without ever discussing or acknowledging the difficulties they had raising children. An apology was certainly never anticipated, as it was not a part of their awareness or vibrational makeup. I learned to release those around me from any expectation at that level. No expectation, no judgment, no disappointment.

Nonetheless, there was an unexpected turn of the icosahedron later in my adult life. Sometime in my thirties, my grandmother and I had a very deep and painful conversation. I was visiting her when she brought up the topic of my childhood—something I had never planned to ever discuss with anyone in the family. She said that she wanted to apologize to me for what she did not do. She told me that she knew, when I was a child, that there was abuse in my house and that she didn't know what to do about it. My grandmother said that although she worried about us, she saw the outcome would break up the family and that she would lose her daughter, as well, in the process. So, she didn't say or do anything. She spoke to me about her deep regret, and her apology was agonizingly sincere and heartfelt. We cried at our own powerlessness at that time. She apologized for not protecting me. I told her that I understood and that I never held her responsible.

It's true; I never once thought this was the shortcoming of anyone in the extended family. Its roots were very much underneath us. I was surprised by my grandmother's apology. What this unexpected apology did for me was important, though. Like the Angels of my childhood, who taught me that I was a child of God, no matter what was happening around me, my grandmother validated my experience. She was an Angel to me that day we talked. I felt seen. I felt heard. I wasn't crazy; this did happen, and it was wrong. My grandmother's apology was a confirmation of the truth of my experience. We now shared the vibration, even twenty or thirty years later; this burden became a bit lighter by bringing it out of the shadows.

Forgiveness in Your Story

There are times during Reiki/energy healing sessions when I am told that the issue the client is experiencing is related to unforgiveness. Sometimes I am guided to speak Ho'Oponopono or to speak apologies to the physical body on behalf of the client. This is not necessarily a spoken-word speech but is often said with the inner voice alongside the healing energies flowing through the client. It requalifies the Reiki energies to the frequency of forgiveness. Sometimes I am shown a glimpse of what this is related to, but more often, when I share this with the client afterward, they recognize exactly what it is related to, or they may even have a vision of a person, time, or place come up in the session, which needed this light work.

Forgiveness, like love, is the healing we so often need. Just like seeking love in the world, we can be healed by finding someone who cares and loves us fully. Even if unloving experiences or abusive relationships were a part of someone's past, flowing with unconditional love can do wonders for the healing of the heart. And so it is, with the miraculous power of forgiveness. How wonderful when someone can be the stand-in for the apologizer, bringing in the vibration of apology, even if they were not a part of the misstep. I call this a **surrogate apology**.

Remember that we do not forgive somebody for them alone. Further, we do not need to wait for the apology, and sometimes it will never come. We forgive someone to set ourselves free. An apology throws the doors wide open, lets the light in, and disperses what was hiding in the shadows.

An apology throws the doors wide open, lets the light in, and disperses what was hiding in the shadows.

In the midst of this "Sorry, not sorry" world, allow me to be that person for you and offer you a healing surrogate apology. I may not have been standing with you at the time of the hurt, but I can shine a light from another place on the icosahedron, illuminating other areas within.

I am sincere, and my words are heartfelt as I "send" the frequencies of apology directly to you, through you, as you read the words now. I pray you receive the energies you need. With a commitment to light and health, *choose to receive* the healing you need, as I provide the surrogate apology below:

Dear beautiful child of Light,
I am sorry that happened to you.
You didn't deserve that; no one does.
Your soul is a loving reflection of light,
and you should have been treated better,
like the precious being, you are.
I regret this.
I am sorry.
Please accept this apology for the
hurt and pain I have caused.
All of it.
I am sorry. Please forgive me.
Thank you.

You might want to read this a few times to really receive the healing vibrations of the surrogate apology. After, take a few moments to scan the four lower bodies – physical, etheric, mental, and emotional. How do you feel? What has changed? How clear is your field?

....

....

....

....

....

....

Forgiveness in the World

To end your journey in the clear place is an admirable goal and a fine destination. After all, you have arrived. In the clear place, you are free from resentment and the pitfalls of judgment. You have successfully cleared your energy field and have effective tools and Angelic guides ready to move disruptive energies out whenever they gather at your door again. Well done. It may be time to put your feet up and enjoy the health, well-being, and freedom that forgiveness offers.

Before you put your stocking feet to rest on the ottoman, let us recall the image of the icosahedron and the crystal-clear light that flows through this geometric gem. The experience of your journey with forgiveness is one triangular aspect of the whole, one of the twenty faces. This clear triangle will inform the rest of the energy of your personal icosahedron quite beautifully. And much personal transformation will follow. However, you are also a part of the collective whole. In the larger world, your life is one triangular piece of humanity's icosahedron. Yes, your personal healing has affected the vibrational fabric of the whole, as all energies (healthy or unhealthy) do. We are grateful for your efforts. But spiritual isolationism is not in alignment with energy. Energy continually flows.

To remain in the clear place, we cannot sit isolated in our

individually-perfected crystal-clear personal atmosphere, thinking it is up to every other individual to find their own crystal-clear place. No. Our shared space of oneness, our interbeing, must extend into the world—in the action we call giving.

The Angels of Forgiveness remind us that to truly receive our healing, we must share it with others, as our lives are not solely ours. Giving and receiving are the same gesture, not sequentially following, but the same, happening at the same time and at the same vibrational intensity. We give. We receive. Forgive. Receive. Clear your personal atmosphere. Clear the world's atmosphere.

> Giving and receiving are the same gesture.

Dear readers and friends, continue to work inwardly. Review the activations found in this book, and allow them to lead to regular actions of health, well-being, and grace. Investigate the core beliefs and shadow thoughts that have been undermining your growth. Learn to identify the pain points lingering within the four lower bodies. Reclaim your health in Divine Strength, Divine Wisdom, and Divine Love. Learn to use your "I am" Presence to heal and transform your life. Learn and practice, and practice, and practice how to forgive every body, every thing. And then . . . share that with the world. Dance. Hum. Sing. Write. Love.

How to Become a Forgiveness Activist

- Be generous with love for yourself and others.
- Be eager to apologize.
- Be quick to forgive.
- As a seeker of truth, quickly admit when you are wrong.
- Placing the value of truth above your personal ego, you will want to honor yourself and others by leaving little or no time between the recognition of truth and the admission of faulty perception.
- Like a fervent activist, demonstrate in the streets. Get comfortable with the following phrases or similar words that easily and lightly acknowledge missteps:
    - "Sorry (friend, mate, sport, love, etc.)."
    - "(Excuse/pardon) me."

- "Oops, my bad."
- When you hear these phrases from others, joyfully release them from your ability to punish.
- Forgive easily, yourself and others.
- Work to release resentments and the need to be correct.
- Flow with forgiveness moment by moment.
- Have compassion for those who:
    - Don't know how to forgive.
    - Don't admit they were wrong.
    - Don't ask for forgiveness.
    - Don't forgive others.
- Recognize that you are an apology surrogate, helping to open long-locked doors for family, friends, and those you meet along the way.
- Demonstrate forgiveness so often that it becomes a part of your human fiber. This is the clear quartz energy of your icosahedron, in action, shining light in the clear place.

I pray that this inner workbook will be a new beginning for you and us, creating the outer change that we know is possible through the grace of forgiveness. Take your place as a forgiveness activist together, and we usher in a new era of forgiveness on the planet.

Glossary of Metaphysical Terms

Angelic Guidance Loving assistance and direction from Divine Messengers.

Angels of Forgiveness A general term used in this book that refers to a collection of Divine Messengers across the spiritual hierarchy (or octaves), including Archangels, Ascended Masters, and the Elohim. These beings have assisted the author in creating this program and book. "They" are available to the reader for the deep work of forgiveness. Some of the specific names of these beautiful beings are recognizable from various religious contexts. Religions are human-made, not Divinely created. Therefore, I am guided not to attach their human-identified names to these pages. Instead, open your uplifted heart to the Divine Energies of Forgiveness and allow the Message to carry the Messenger(s) to you without your preconception.

Ascended Masters Beings who have lived lifetimes in embodiment on Earth, who have successfully raised their vibrational frequencies to return to the fullness of Higher Self—whole and complete and no longer limited by time and space. They hold the Divine Plan or Divine Order and are available to aid human beings on their journeys of ascension as Master Teachers or Chohans.

Brow chakra (third eye chakra) *See* **Chakra system**

Chakra system Chakra is a Sanskrit word meaning "wheel," referring to the energy centers found within and around the energy body of all living beings. The separation of the chakras, by vibrational frequency and color, marks the unhealed system. Ultimately, when all frequencies work together in harmony and all colors reunite into one white light, true healing of separation occurs, and ascension begins.

Working from the feet to the head, the chakras are as follows:

- **Earth Star chakra:** Southernmost chakra, located (24 inches) beneath the feet, connecting you to the ascending life force energy available to you from Mother Earth. Your southern axis and the base of the Merkaba structure around you.

- **Root chakra:** Located at the base of the spine, this energy center represents your sense of belonging, security, and right work.

- **Sacral chakra:** Located in the lower abdomen and the area of the low back and pelvis. This represents your passion, creativity, and sexuality/sensuality.

- **Solar plexus chakra:** Located in the upper abdomen, at the area of the stomach, liver, pancreas, and digestive system. This is the center of your strength, will, and human emotion.

- **Heart chakra:** The center of love that holds the energetic imprint of all the love you have known throughout your lifetimes.

- **High Heart chakra:** A vibrational chamber that is an octave "above" the heart chakra and holds your "I am" Presence and the Three-Fold Flame.

- **Throat chakra:** Located in the throat and neck area and is the energetic center of communication in all forms: verbal, written, physical, and psychic.

- **Zeal chakra:** A vibrational octave "above" the throat chakra; this is the center of communication with the Divine.

- **Brow chakra (third eye chakra):** The area of the forehead activated by the opening of the pineal gland in the center of the brain. It is the center of insight, intuition, and inner vision.

- **Corona chakra:** The energy center at the top of the head, also known as the crown chakra. This is the area of the Flame of Enlightenment and higher consciousness.

- **Soul Star chakra:** The northernmost chakra and the top of the Merkaba surround the lower bodies. This is the pathway of higher consciousness into the four lower bodies. This chakra is the lower chakra of your Higher Self.

Chi Universal life force energy and animating principle that flows through all living beings. Also referred to as Ki or Ti.

Chohan A spiritual teacher; Maha Chohan, meaning master teacher, is also called Holy Spirit.

Chord A musical term referring to the entwined relationship of two or more notes played at once.

Collective field The shared energy field of all living beings.

Cords The energetic attachments connected to other people, times, and places that will keep us bound to other energies, whether we are aware of them or not.

Corona chakra *See* **Chakra system**

Cut cords Release of unwanted attachment to other people, times, and places, usually conducted by a trained spiritual healer or shaman, to release the energy so it will return to wherever it belongs. Love is never cut, as it belongs to the Divine Consciousness.

Detachment A conscious choice to release the energy you hold that belongs to others and to recall your own life force, lovingly setting yourself and all others free.

Divine A term used to describe God, Source, or Creator.

Divine Order A term used to refer to the Creator's Plan for humanity, also known as Divine Plan or the Immaculate Construct.

Earth Star chakra *See* **Chakra system**

Elementals Divine Beings that reside within the forces of nature to assist humanity and preserve the planet. They respond to human emotions and have, thusly, been imprisoned in grotesque physical forms or are kept out of sight through disbelief and stories of their ridiculous or dangerous natures. They are generally found in the following forms:

- **Fire:** salamanders, snakes, dragons, and all representations of the lizard kingdom
- **Air:** sylphs, wisps, and winged fairies
- **Earth:** nature spirits, devas, gnomes, elves, and leprechauns
- **Water:** undines, sea creatures/monsters, and mer-beings

Elohim The creative energies and aspects of God flowing to the Earth along the Great Rays.

Energetic field, *See* **Collective field**

Flower of Life The sacred geometric shape of intersecting and overlapping circles, each one sharing the purity of the Divine Plan between them. This is used in this book to illustrate the transfer of energy through the collective field, thusly becoming the "Flow-er of Life."

Great Rays The metaphysical term used to describe the vibrational aspects of the Great Light of the Divine Creator, as the Energy created matter. These Energies are held by Divine Beings who maintain these qualities for all creation. Although there are twelve Great Rays, eight are available for lightwork in proper use and connection. These eight rays/flames of light hold Divine qualities such as strength, wisdom, love, purity, truth and healing, peace, freedom, and integration.

Great Sun The higher octave, the Divine Presence, of our solar sun, sometimes referred to as the sun behind the sun, the Soular Sun. Esoteric texts refer to this as the home of the Creator, in Sirius.

Hardwiring The concept from evolutionary psychology which acknowledges that although human beings have their individuality, as a whole, we have been indoctrinated into our limiting beliefs about ourselves through our genes, inherited traits, and by those who have gone before us, teaching us what it is to be human. The Angels of Forgiveness suggest that we may not be operating from Divine Truth but from inherited limitations, known as hardwiring. The opening of the zeal chakra is imperative to undo this hardwiring.

Heart chakra *See* **Chakra system**

Heart chamber *See* **Chakra system**, **High Heart chakra**

Higher Self The refined part of you that remains in spirit, fully ascended, and aware of your soul contract, life plan, and is over-lighting your current embodiment.

High Heart chakra *See* **Chakra system**

"I am" Presence The Divine Presence within each of us and the space within the High Heart chakra that holds this spark/flame of the Divine. The words "I Am" are considered a call, or activation, of the Creator-God within. It is an acknowledgment that you are co-creating this energetic experience of life. Whatever you say after "I am" becomes an activation, a calling-in of that energy, whether intentional or not. Each of us is the Divine Presence in action.

Inner light This refers to the Divine Presence, represented by Infinite Light, within all living beings.

Karma A Law of Life that acknowledges individual free will. The individual has a responsibility to the whole, for every energetic vibration will ultimately need to be brought back into balance and harmony by the one who initially sent the energy out.

Karmic burden The responsibility the individual has to the whole. Whatever is sent out into the **collective field** has your unique energetic imprint on it and belongs to you. You will need to requalify all disharmonious frequencies that contain your energetic imprint.

Karmic resolution This is the release of the karmic burden.

Kinesphere The circle of energy surrounding you as if you were a planet. Rudolf Laban first used this term in his movement theory and practice to describe the spherical space around the body whose periphery can be reached easily with extended limbs.

Law of Forgiveness This law represents the larger Law of Life, which is karma. Forgiveness is received to the degree it is given as we participate in there balance of energies.

Law of Life These underlying Divine Principles govern the physical, etheric, mental, and emotional constructs of all living beings. These are not laws of man, institutions, or governments but the Divine Order of the Creator. It is what scientists and metaphysicians seek to discover and uncover.

Law of Vibration Like vibrates like.

Lifestream The energetic flow of time and space during one's experience of embodiment. This term goes beyond the usual concept of "lifetime," as it includes previous and subsequent incarnations of the soul.

Lightworkers This is a broad term to describe those working individually to raise the collective consciousness of humanity on its path homeward through ascension.

Lizard kingdom, see Elementals (fire)

Mantra This is a Sanskrit word meaning an instrument of thought. It is a spoken word form that is used to aid in meditation. It is generally repeated so that the energies held within the words will fill the four lower bodies of the one speaking the mantra, unlocking deeper wisdom held within the word or phrase.

Maya A metaphysical term describing the illusory nature of matter.

Merkaba A Hebrew term (also, Merkabah/Merkavah) meaning chariot. In sacred geometry, it is the structure surrounding the lower bodies, made of two intersecting tetrahedrons (pyramids). The top pyramid is the masculine/electrical energy; the lower pyramid is the feminine/magnetic energy. This structure is in constant motion, holding the four lower bodies, the auric field, and the personal akashic records. It is creating and balancing the electromagnetic field of the body through the movement of the torus. The northernmost point is at the Soul Star chakra; the southernmost point is at the Earth Star chakra.

Reiki Pronounced *ray-key*, this Japanese term means universal life force energy and the healing practice that uses it. There are many forms of Reiki (perhaps close to a hundred). The Reiki practice described in this book was received by Dr. Usui and utilizes channeled Divine healing energy to assist in healing the four lower bodies of the recipient.

Reiki Master Teacher A term used by western Reiki practitioners and therapists who have obtained a substantial level of skill and practice with Reiki, completed their formal training, and are now capable of teaching and passing attunements to others.

Root chakra *See* **Chakra system**

Sacral chakra *See* **Chakra system**

Solar plexus chakra *See* **Chakra system**

Soul Star chakra *See* **Chakra system**

Shadow thoughts These are thoughtforms that are working "behind the scenes." They are unresolved and often represent your core beliefs and subconscious desires, ultimately affecting your outcomes.

Spiritual Activism A practice of working in the physical world from a metaphysical impulse, making manifest in the material that which is spiritual, consciously bringing spiritual light to physical matters.

Surrogate apology The act of standing in for the apologizer, giving a loving voice to the apology (which may never come from the one who caused harm) to assist in the healthy forgiveness process. One who conducts surrogate apology for others is an **Apology surrogate.**

Theosophical Mystics This branch of Theosophy was developed in the latter part of the nineteenth century and formally named by Helena Blavatsky. Theosophical Mysticism seeks truth beyond personal revelation and religious belief systems, seeking to find Divine Wisdom within occult science and metaphysical investigation.

Thoughtforms The energies made manifest through our thoughts, whether intentional or not, as thoughts become form.

Three-Fold Flame The Divine Presence within all of mankind within the **High Heart chakra.** This is a single Flame with three aspects or vibrational qualities: blue/Divine Strength, gold/Divine Wisdom, and pink/Divine Love.

Throat chakra *See* **Chakra system**

Torus The energetic shape created by the electromagnetic flow of energy around all living things. It is a geometric structure created by the flow from an inner opening, moving outward from the center and returning in an upward magnetic pull back up through the center.

Violet Flame A tool of transformation and healing available to all who ask for its presence to uplift any person, place, or situation. Many have a daily practice of calling in the Violet Flame to surround themselves, their intentions, and even the

planet for the highest and best for all.
Zeal chakra *See* **Chakra system**

Bibliography

Alfred, J. *Our Invisible Bodies: Scientific Evidence for Subtle Bodies.* Indiana: Trafford Publishing, 2006.

Andrews, T. *Sacred Sounds.* Woodbury, Minnesota: Llewellyn, 1992.

Bach, E. *The Essential Writings of Dr. Edward Bach.* London: Vermilion, 1933/2005.

Bailey, A. *The Consciousness of the Atom.* New York: Lucis Publishing Company, 1922/2000.

_____. *The Rays and The Initiations.* New York: Lucis Publishing Company, 1960.

_____. *The Reappearance of the Christ.* New York: Lucis Publishing Company, 1948.

Ball, S. *Bloom: Using Flower Essences for Personal Development and Spiritual Growth.* London: Vermilion, 2006.

Becker, R. & Selden, G. *The Body Electric: Electromagnetism and the Foundation of Life.* New York: William Morrow, 1998.

Bodin, L., Bodin, N. & Graciet, J. *The Book of Ho'Oponopono: The Hawaiian Practice of Forgiveness and Healing.* Rochester, Vermont: Destiny Books, 2012/2016.

Born, M. *The Born-Einstein Letters, 1916-1955: Friendship, Politics and Physics in Uncertain Times.* London: Palgrave Macmillan, 2005.

Bowley, F. *Brave Intuitive Painting.* Beverly, Massachusettes Quarry Books, 2012.

Blavatsky, H. *The Secret Doctrine: The Synthesis of Science, Religion, and Philosophy, Vols 1 & 2.* Epub: Library of Alexandria, 2012.

Brennan, B. *Hands of Light: A Guide to Healing Through the Human Energy Field.* New York: Bantam, 1988.

Cheney, M. *Tesla: Man Out of Time.* New York: Simon & Schuster, 1981.

Childre, D. & Martin, H. *The Heartmath Solution.* San Francisco: HarperOne, 2000.

Ciesco, D. *Your True Voice: Tools to Embrace a Fully-Expressed Life.*

Winchester, UK: Ayni Books, 2014.

Clerc, O. *The Gift of Forgiveness.* Rochester, Vermont: Findhorn Press, 2010.

Cousto, H. *The Cosmic Octave.* California: LifeRhythm, 2000.

Dalai Lama [Gyatso, T.], Goleman, D. (ed). *Healing Emotions: Conversations with the Dalai Lama on Psychology, Meditation, and the Mind-Body Connection.* Colorado: Shambhala, 1997.

Dalai Lama [Gyatso, T.], Houshmand, A., Livingston, R. & Wallaces, B. (eds.). *Where Buddhism Meets Neuroscience: Conversations with the Dalai Lama on the Spiritual and Scientific Views of Our Minds.* Colorado: Shambhala, 1999.

Durand, A. *Illumination of the Shadow: Ancestral Wisdom from the Past for the Future.* UK: Shamanism & Evolving Consciousness Ltd., 2020.

Emoto, M. *The Hidden Messages in Water.* Hillsboro, Oregon: Beyond Words Publishing, 2004.

Feldenkrais, M. *Awareness Through Movement.* New York: HarperOne, 1990.

Gaynor, M. *The Healing Power of Sound.* Boston: Shambhala, 2002.

Gerber, R. *Vibrational Medicine.* Vermont: Bear & Company, 2001.

Godwin, J (ed). *Cosmic Music: Musical Keys to the Interpretation of Reality.* Rochester, Vermont: Inner Traditions International, 1989.

Godwin, J. *Harmonies of Heaven and Earth: Mysticism in Music, from Antiquity to the Avant-Garde.* Rochester, Vermont: Inner Traditions International, 1995

_____. *The Harmony of the Spheres: A Sourcebook of the Pythagorean Tradition in Music.* Rochester, Vermont: Inner Traditions International, 1993.

Goldman, J. *Healing Sounds: The Power of Harmonics.* Rochester, Vermont: Healing Arts Press, 2002.

Great Divine Director. *The "I Am" Discourses.* Illinois: St. Germain Press, 2001.

Hall, J. *The Encyclopedia of Crystals.* Beverly, Massachusetts: Fair Winds Press, 2006.

Hall, M. *Mythology I: Stories and Symbols of the Sacred.* Los Angeles: The Philosophical Research Society, 2021.

_____. *Occult Anatomy: The Body as Symbol.* Los Angeles: The Philosophical Research Society, 2021.

Halprin, A. & Kaplan, R. *Making Dances That Matter.* Connecticut: Wesleyan University Press, 2019.

Halprin, A. *Movement Ritual.* San Francisco: San Francisco Dancers' Workshop, 1981.

_____. *Returning to Health: With Dance, Movement & Imagery.* California: LifeRhythm, 2002.

Halprin, D. *The Expressive Body in Life, Art and Therapy.* UK: Jessica Kingsley Publishers, 2003.

Hampes, W. "The Relationship Between Humor Styles and Forgiveness." National Institutes for Health (NIH), National Library of Medicine. https://www.ncbi.nlm.nih.gov, 2016.

Hawkins, E. *The Body is a Clear Place: and Other Statements on Dance.* Princeton, New Jersey: Dance Horizons, 1992.

Hay, D. *My Body, the Buddhist.* Hanover, New Hampshire: Wesleyan University Press, 2000.

Hay, L. *You Can Heal Your Life.* California: Hay House, 2004.

Herringshaw, T.W. (ed). *Local and National Poets of America: With Interesting Biographical Sketches.* Chicago: American Publishers' Association, 1890.

Holmes, E. *The Science of Mind.* New York: Tarcher/Penguin, 1929.

Howard, J. *The Bach Flower Remedies Step by Step.* London: Vermilion, 2005.

Huang, C. & Lynch, J. *Thinking Body, Dancing Mind.* New York: Bantam, 1994.

Hubert, C. *That Which You Are Seeking is Causing You to Seek.* California: Keep It Simple Books, 1990.

Jones, T. *Dictionary of the Bach Flower Remedies: Positive and Negative Aspects.* London: Vermilion, 1995.

Anodea, J. & Vega, S. *The Sevenfold Journey: Reclaiming Mind, Body & Spirit Through the Chakras.* New York: Crossing Press, 1993.

Kaminski, P. & Katz, R. *Flower Essence Repertory: A Comprehensive*

Guide to the Flower Essences Researched by Dr. Edward Bach and by the Flower Essence Society. California: Flower Essence Society, 2015,

Keyes, L. *Toning: The Creative and Healing Power of the Voice.* California: DeVorss Publications, 2008.

King, G. R. *The I Am Discourses, The Ascended Master Saint Germain through Godfrey Ray King.* Illinois: Saint Germain Press, 1935/2013.

King, G. R. *Unveiled Mysteries.* Illinois: St. Germain Press, 1973.

Levine, S. *Becoming Kuan Yin: The Evolution of Compassion.* San Francisco: Weiser Books, 2013.

Lipton, B. *The Biology of Belief: Unleashing the Power of Consciousness, Matter, and Miracles.* New York: Hay House, 2005.

Luk, A.D.K. *Law of Life and Teachings by Divine Beings: Books I, II, & III.* Colorado: A.D.K. Luk Publications, 1978/1994.

McKusick, E. *Tuning the Human Biofield: Healing with Vibrational Sound Therapy.* Rochester, Vermont: Healing Arts Press, 2014.

McLaren, K. *Your Aura and Your Chakras: The Owner's Manual.* San Francisco: Weiser Books, 1998.

Melody. *Love is in the Earth: A Kaleidoscope of Crystals.* Colorado: Earth-Love Publishing, 1995.

Moss, R. *The Mandala of Being: Discovering the Power of Awareness.* California: New World Library, 2007.

Müller, F (trans.) *Dhammapada.* Project Gutenberg, 2017. http//www.gutenberg.org/2/0/1/2017

Myss, C. *Anatomy of the Spirit: The Seven Stages of Power and Healing.* New York: Harmony, 1997.

Pogacnik, M. *Nature Spirits & Elemental Beings: Working with the Intelligence in Nature.* Rochester, Vermont: Findhorn Press, 2009.

Prophet, E. & Spadaro, P. *Your Seven Energy Centers: A Holistic Approach to Physical, Emotional and Spiritual Vitality.* Montana: Summit University Press, 2000.

Prophet, M. & Prophet, E. *Lords of the Seven Rays.* Montana: Summit University Press: 1986.

_____. *The Masters and Their Retreats.* Montana: Summit

University Press, 2003.

_____. *Saint Germain On Alchemy.* Montana: Summit University Press, 1985/1993.

Pythagoras. *The Golden Verses of Pythagoras and Other Pythagorean Fragments.* Nevada: Forgotten Books, 1904/2007.

Quest, P. *The Reiki Manual.* New York: Tarcher/Penguin, 2011.

Schroeder, W. (ed). *Electrons: The Building Blocks of the Universe and The Elemental Kingdom.* Mount Shasta, California: Ascended Master Teaching Foundation, 2008.

Schucman, H. (scribe). *A Course in Miracles.* California: Foundations for Inner Peace, 1976.

Shakespeare.W. *The Merchant of Venice*, Harbio, essex, England: Longman, 1994

Simmons, R. *The Alchemy of Stones: Co-Creating with Crystals, Minerals, and Gemstones for Healing and Transformation.* Rochester, Vermont: Destiny Books, 2020.

Simmons, R & Naisha A. *The Book of Stones: Who They Are & What They Teach.* Vermont: Heaven & Earth Publishing, 2007.

Stein, D. *Essential Reiki: A Complete Guide to an Ancient Healing Art.* New York: Crossing Press, 1995.

Stewart, D. *The Chemistry of Essential Oils Made Simple.* Missouri: Care Publications, 2016.

Strohmeier, J. & Westbrook, P. *Divine Harmony: The Life and Teachings of Pythagoras.* Rockville, Maryland: Harmonia Books, 2012.

Tesla, N. "The Problem of Increasing Human Energy," *The Century Illustrated Monthly Magazine,* June 1900.

Tesla, N. Major, D. (ed). *My Inventions.* San Bernardino, California: The Philovox, 1919/2013.

Torok, L. "Here and Now: Reiki Grounding and the Earth Star Chakra," *Reiki News Magazine,* vol 20, issue 4, Winter 2021.

Tutu, D. & Tutu, M. *The Book of Forgiving.* New York: HarperOne, 2014.

Usui, M. & Arjava Petter, F. *The Original Reiki Handbook of Dr. Mikao Usui.* Twin Lakes, Wisconsin: Lotus Press, 2011.

Vanzant, I. *Forgiveness: 21 Days to Forgive Everyone for Everything.*

California: Hay House, 2013.

Weiss, P.& Taruskin, R. (eds.) *Music in the Western World: A History in Documents.* California: Schirmer Cengage, 2008.

Wheeler, F.J. *The Bach Remedies Repertory.* London: Vermilion, 1952/1996.

Williamson, M. *A Return to Love.* San Francisco: HarperOne, 1996.

Yamaguchi, T. *Light on the Origins of Reiki.* Twin Lakes, Wisconsin: Lotus Press, 2007.

Yogananda, P. *Karma and Reincarnation.* Nevada City: Crystal Clarity Publishers, 2007.

Index

A

Activations
about, 10–11
acknowledging pain, 23–24
call and response, 190–191
cutting cords, 178–179
dance, 88–89
eight breaths, 96
etheric body exploration, 80–81
fire of forgiveness, 134–135
"I am" breathing, 140–142
laugh laboratory, 200–201
Mother Earth, 158–159
role models, 42–43
squared breath, 29–31
sunset journey, 176
toning, 189–190
truth, 123–124
waning moon journey, 176–177
willing to forgive, 177–178
Air
breathing and, 139–142

creation and, 140
forgiving thoughtform, 142–145
Amethyst, 133, 153, 164, 165
Angelic guidance, 112, 233
Angels of Forgiveness
about, 4, 19–20, 233
Anti-love, 47
Apologies, 93, 97, 157, 225–228, 239
Apology surrogate, 239
Archaean butterstone, 154
Ascended masters, 5, 233
Attunements, 105
Auric egg, 6

B

Bach, Edward, 166, 167
Blame, 93–94
Blavatsky, H.P., 6, 239
The Body is a Clear Place (Hawkins), 80
Boethius, 193–194
Breathing, 139–142
Brow Chakra, 234

C

Catholic Church, 108
Chakra system, 77–79, 151, 233–235
Chi, 103, 235
Childhood traumas, 18
Childre, Doc, 129
Chohan, 5, 235
Chord, 191, 235
Clear place, 13, 215–220
Collective field, 9, 235
Connectedness, 6
Cords, 25, 178–179, 235
Corona chakra, 234
A Course in Miracles, 205
Crown chakra. See Corona chakra
Crystals
amethyst, 133, 153, 164, 165
archaean butterstone, 154
clearing, 152
diopside, 153, 165
fuschite, 154, 165
gold, 154
green muscovite, 154

quartz, 164, 165
rose quartz, 152–
153, 164, 165
selenite, 131, 132,
152, 164, 165
working with,
152–155, 158–159
Cubes, 149

D

Detachment, 95,
111–112, 235
Dhammapada, 37
Diopside, 153, 165
Divine, 130, 235
Divine Order, 39, 57,
235
Dodecahedron, 185,
189

E

Earth
earth star chakra
and, 150–151
essential oils,
155–157
grounding and,
149–150
working with
crystals, 152–155
Earth Star chakra, 48,
49, 66, 150–151,
153, 234
Einstein, Albert, 25
Electromagnetic field,
25–26, 48, 84–86
Elementals, 9, 131,
139, 149, 163,

188–189, 235
Elements, 130
See also specific
types
Elohim, 133, 236
Emotional body
described, 7–8, 9
putting up walls,
185–187
Emotions, suppressed,
47
Empaths, 33–37
Energetic cords, 25,
178–179, 235
Energy body. *See*
Etheric body
Energy field, 28, 29,
35, 41, 78, 86, 105,
130
Essential oils, 155–157
Etheric body, 6–7, 9,
25, 77–84, 88–89

F

Family stories, 86–87
Family tree healing. See
Generational healing
Field. See Energy field
Fire
about, 129
color frequencies, 133
mystic and, 130–
131
sacred fire energy,
131–132
Violet Flame, 133
Flower essences,
166–168

Flower of Life, 27, 28,
236
Forgiveness
crystals for, 152–
155
daily, 93
essential oils for,
155–157
etheric body and,
82–84
judgment and,
58–59
law of, 38–39, 210,
237
light of, 56–57
suffering and, 39–41
superficial, 5, 186
wheel of, 94–96
Forgiveness activism,
229–230
Forgiving thoughtform,
142–145
4GiveNess Project
about, 10
clear place
meditation, 215–
219
every body, every
thing meditation,
171–175
garden of truth
meditation, 65–70
temple of truth
meditation, 117–
122
zeal of truth
meditation, 205–
210

Four lower bodies, 5–8, 57–58, 60, 93, 164, 175, 238
Frankincense, 156
Free will, 48, 112, 151, 154
Fuschite, 154, 165

G
Garden of truth meditation, 65–70
Gems
gem baths, 164–165
gem elixirs, 165
working with, 152–155
Generational healing, 84–88, 104
Gold, 154
Great Rays, 130, 133, 236
Great Sun, 236
Green Muscovite, 154
Grounding, 149–150
Guided meditations. *See* Meditations

H
Hardwiring, 111, 236
Hawkins, Erick, 80
Hay, Louise, 33
Heart center, 130, 142
Heart chakra, 57, 234
The Heartmath Solution (Childre and Martin), 129
Higher Self, 236

High Heart chakra, 57, 234, 239
Ho'Oponopono, 96–100

I
"I am" Presence, 236–237
Icosahedron, 1–3, 15, 163, 228
Inner light, 237
Irritation, feelings of, 55–57

J
Judgment, 58–59, 61, 209

K
Karma, 84–86, 237
Karmic burden, 9, 85–86, 237
Karmic resolution, 237
Kinesphere, 150, 237
Kinesthetic sense, 79

L
Laban, Rudolf, 237
Laughter, 199–201
Lavender essential oil, 157
Law of Forgiveness, 38–39, 210, 237
Law of Life, 237
Law of vibration, 8, 22, 26–27, 237
Lifestream, 129, 237
Light body. *See* Etheric body

Lightworkers, 133, 238
Living Inherent Force Energy (LIFE), 156
Lizard kingdom, 131, 235
Love is in the Earth (Melody), 154
Lower bodies, 5–8, 57–58, 60, 93, 164, 175, 238

M
Mantras, 56–58, 97–100, 238
Martin, Howard, 129
Matryoshka, 6–7
Maya, 86, 238
Meditations
garden of truth, 65–70
with Ho'Oponopono, 99–100
temple of truth, 117–122
Memory body. *See* Etheric body
Mental body, 7, 8–9
The Merchant of Venice (Shakespeare), 194–195
Merkaba, 172–173, 238
Minerals, 152–155
Music, 187, 198
Music of the Spheres, 193

N

Nature devas, 149, 158

O

Octahedrons, 139

P

Pain
  judgment and, 58–59
  perception of, 20–22
  phantom pain, 24
  suppressed emotions and, 47
Phantom pain, 24
Physical body, 5–6, 9
Pink Flame, 132
Platonic solids, 1–3, 129, 139, 149, 163, 185, 189
Playlist, 198
Prayers
  awakening in forgiveness, 221
  family tree, 87–88
  forgiveness for the world, 212
  release of judgment, 61
Pyramids, 129
Pythagoras, 193, 194

Q

Quartz, 164, 165

R

Radio City Rockettes, 31–33
Reiki
  about, 103–106
  attunements, 105
  defined, 238
  detachment and, 111–112
  etheric body and, 78
  for forgiveness, 113
  intentions and, 109–110
  for self-healing, 106–107
Reiki Master Teacher, 104, 238
Religions, 107–109
Resonance, 26
Role models, 42–43
Roman chamomile essential oil, 157
Root chakra, 234
Rose essential oil, 156
Rose quartz, 152–153, 164, 165
Rudra Mudra, 134, 135
Russian nesting dolls, 6–7

S

Sacral chakra, 163, 196, 234
Sacred geometry, 1, 238
Salamanders, 131, 235
Selenite, 131, 132, 152, 164, 165

Shadow thoughts, 50–51, 239
Shakespeare, William, 193, 194–195
Shame, 93–94
Simeona, Mornnah Nalamaku, 96–97
639Hz frequency, 196–197
Solar plexus chakra, 123, 131, 134, 234
Soul Star chakra, 66–67, 234–235
Sound
  as frequency, 187
  for healing, 189
  laughter and, 199–201
  music and, 187, 198
  Music of the Spheres, 193
  as natural force, 188
  639Hz frequency, 196–197
Spiritual Activism, 11, 239
St. Germain, 133
Suffering, 39–41
Suppressed emotions, 47
Surrogate apology, 226–228, 239

T

Tangerine essential oil, 157

Temple of Truth
    meditation, 117–
    122, 173
Tesla, Nikola, 28–29
Theosophical Mystics,
    6, 239
Third eye chakra, 234
Thoughtforms, 7, 239
Three-fold flame, 57,
    118, 239
Throat chakra, 234
Torus, 25–26, 239
Truth, 123–124

U
Undines, 163
Unified field, 85–86

V
Victim's mentality, 93
Violet Flame, 133, 153,
    239–240
W
Water
    about, 163
    flower essences,
    166–168
    gem baths and
    elixirs, 164–165
Wheel of forgiveness,
    94–96
Willingness, 156

Z
Zeal chakra, 206, 234,
    236

Gratitude

We find ourselves in a classroom without desks, textbooks, or chalkboards—only other students. I am grateful for my classmates and those enrolled in the " life " course with me. This book contains *my* notes from the forgiveness class, and I am honored to share them with the next grade levels. Admittedly, I didn't get A's in all the classes; I struggled in most of them. May they be helpful study guides, and may you pass every test.

I wish to thank those who call me family, my parents, of both trees—the tree with whom I shared my life and the tree with whom I share my genetics. I want to thank my siblings of both family trees, with whom time and space were limited. I want to thank my friends (of all grade levels) who took various classes with me. Thank you for sharing your notes lovingly with me.

My true teachers have been my spiritual guides, the Angels of Forgiveness. They are a diverse collection of beings, some of whom have names you may be familiar with, some only a distant recollection from neighboring "long-ago" belief systems. This is not the book to make such introductions; perhaps that will follow at another time. Nonetheless, I thank the Angels of Forgiveness for their steady and ongoing guidance, love, patience, and friendship. This book simply would not exist without them.

Thank you to the dancers of Avocado Dance Theatre, who fearlessly created the first "Journey to a Clear Place" with me to explore forgiveness in theatrical dance and a seaside film. Your courage and willingness to be vulnerable inspired me to go deeper.

My heartfelt thanks to friends and family who offered encouragement. I'm not sure you realize how much your words and support have inspired and helped me complete this work. Thank you Zoe for your tech wizardry

Thank you to Anne Watson for her photography, and to

my editor, Sandy Draper, for her expertise, guidance, and encouragement. Gratitude to Catherine Murray of Piggle Design for her creativity and design. Thank you Sandy Blood for the immense task of indexing.

I wish to acknowledge the support I received from the Hay House Writers' Community and the excellent resources they provide.

Lastly, but most significantly, I want to thank my husband, Steve Torok, for his love, support, and willingness to regularly explore new avenues and the process of forgiveness with me. Thank you for the music.

Blessings to all.

About the Author

M. Lori Torok has been an empathic communicator, attuned to the angelic realms since childhood. Her mystical connections have developed to where she can assist others in the healing of physical, emotional, mental, and spiritual energetic disruptions. She enthusiastically teaches others how to recall and develop these gifts of higher communication directly for themselves.

In 2018, Lori was directed by the Angels of Forgiveness to create a program called "The 4GiveNess Project" to help humanity learn how to forgive every one, every thing. This program has evolved for those wanting to grow in understanding and skill as they walk the journey of forgiveness.

M. Lori Torok is an alternative health practitioner and owner of Eloia Healing Arts at Temecula Reiki & Sound Therapy, a thriving practice in Southern California. Lori is dedicated to assisting humanity in raising their personal and collective vibrations for spiritual wellness, health, and happiness.

She has a bachelor's degree from Niagara University and a Master of Arts from the State University of New York at Brockport. She is a Bach Foundation Registered Practitioner who studied flower essence therapy at the Bach Centre in Wallingford, England. Lori is an ordained minister and a non-denominational celebrant. She writes for online publications such as *New Earth Consciousness* and *Know Thyself, Heal Thyself* and has published articles in print for *Reiki News Magazine*.

Before her present work, Lori was a Rockette with Radio City Music Hall and a college professor, for over seventeen years, at the University of Alabama at Birmingham and at Mt. San Jacinto College, where she was chair of Theatre Arts and Dance.

Websites:

www.M.LoriTorok.com

www.EloiaHealingArts.com